The
Good Mother
Myth

ALSO BY NANCY REDDY

Pocket Universe

The Long Devotion: Poets Writing Motherhood (coeditor)

Acadiana

Double Jinx

The
Good Mother
Myth

*Unlearning Our Bad Ideas About
How to Be a Good Mom*

....

Nancy Reddy

ST. MARTIN'S PRESS
NEW YORK

First published in the United States by St. Martin's Press,
an imprint of St. Martin's Publishing Group

THE GOOD MOTHER MYTH. Copyright © 2024 by Nancy Reddy.
All rights reserved. Printed in the United States of America.
For information, address St. Martin's Publishing Group,
120 Broadway, New York, NY 10271.

www.stmartins.com

Library of Congress Cataloging-in-Publication Data

Names: Reddy, Nancy, 1982- author.
Title: The good mother myth : unlearning our bad ideas about
    how to be a good mom / Nancy Reddy.
Description: First edition. | New York : St. Martin's Press, 2025. |
    Includes bibliographical references and index.
Identifiers: LCCN 2024034015 | ISBN 9781250336644 (hardcover) |
    ISBN 9781250336651 (ebook)
Subjects: LCSH: Motherhood—Social aspects. | Motherhood—Psychological
    aspects. | Motherhood—Public opinion.
Classification: LCC HQ759 .R454 2025 | DDC 306.874/3—dc23/
    eng/20240731
LC record available at https://lccn.loc.gov/2024034015

Our books may be purchased in bulk for promotional, educational,
or business use. Please contact your local bookseller or the Macmillan Corporate
and Premium Sales Department at 1-800-221-7945, extension 5442,
or by email at MacmillanSpecialMarkets@macmillan.com.

First Edition: 2025

10 9 8 7 6 5 4 3 2 1

For every mom who's wondered if she's good enough.
You're already doing great.

If you're a new parent and you're struggling, you deserve to get help. Postpartum Support International—1-800-944-4773 or www.postpartum.net—is a good place to start.

Contents

Introduction

"Love Is a Wondrous State"

Before I had a baby I was good at things.

I was a graduate student in a competitive program, barreling on into a PhD in English after finishing an MFA in poetry. I raced through my coursework, completing the required classes in two years instead of the usual three. I defended my doctoral exams at thirty-six weeks pregnant, then went home to paint the office-turned-nursery, wobbling on a stepstool as I reached to coat even the ceiling in the palest gray blue so that the tiny room was transformed into a jewel box of fresh color. I prepared for motherhood with the same discipline I'd used for every other hard thing in my life. I believed that I could handle any challenge if I worked hard enough, read the right books, consulted the experts and followed their advice.

This was one of the myths I had absorbed from the mommy blogs and the parenting advice books I consumed alongside my prenatal vitamins and leafy greens throughout my pregnancy: that motherhood was an individual pursuit at which I could excel, in the same way that I had excelled in school, in my chosen profession of academia, in the creation of a picture-perfect life for myself—one in which I believed a child would fit perfectly, by dint of my careful planning and preparation.

At the same time, there was another part of me that believed in some kind of magic: another myth, this one of a transformation beyond even the one that I could plan and study my way toward. My whole life, years before becoming a mother myself, I'd heard women talk about the automatic, selfless love of motherhood. "It's like seeing your heart walking around outside your body," more than one had told me, as earnestly as if they'd just discovered the cliché themselves. But as a poet, I'd been taught to distrust clichés. Were they saying it because that's what everyone else said? Had their babies turned their brains to mush? And yet, I craved the simplicity of this sentiment, however sticky sweet. "When you have your own, you'll understand," they told me, and I thought maybe I would. The idea that I'd become a good mother through some mystical combination of hormones and instinct was so deeply embedded, I couldn't even recognize it as the myth it was.

I'd spent years looking at the women around me for models of what it meant to be a good mother. The women I saw around town, the mothers I'd watched surreptitiously for years, made it look effortless. My husband and I had moved to Madison, Wisconsin, the archetypal college town with its array of cute cafés, wide bike lanes, and restaurants boasting more than thirty local beers on tap, for my graduate program. In our years there, I'd absorbed the message of attachment parenting, which seemed to hover in the very air above the kombucha and the quinoa at the co-op: natural is best. All around me—at the farmers market, the sidewalk cafés that bloomed each spring when the lakes unfroze, on the bus, even—blissed-out mothers strolled with peaceful babies cradled in carriers against their chests. (It was nearly always the mothers, though occasionally you'd see a bearded baby-wearing dad looking very proud of his progressive parenting. Those men always seemed somehow to wear the baby in the Ergo in italics, like an ad for a *good feminist dad*.) Their babies had whimsical cloth-patterned diapers. The mothers had bright silicone necklaces that doubled as teethers for their babies. They talked intently about the bonding brought on by nursing, the benefits of co-sleeping. When the babies whimpered or rustled, the mothers knew how to decode their complaints and calm them before they turned to cries. A third myth: motherhood, when done right, could be easy.

My own mother had been fierce—less hazy glow and more iron will, but still endlessly devoted. I remember her, in her lean single-mother days, when she took the bus to her office downtown and cooked pot pies from recipes off the back of the Bisquick box, declaring, "I would eat dog food for you." I'd taken that to mean that being a mother meant always putting your children first and never minding, never noticing that your dinner was the scraps from their plates. Another core myth of motherhood: that you—that I—would love your kids so much that all your own desires would just fall away. I'd believed that love would be easy and natural. I knew that caring for a child would be work, but I expected that the overwhelming, instant love I'd surely feel would make it so all that caregiving didn't really feel like labor.

But then I was a mother, and I did mind. I hadn't been made milder, willing to give up sleep, ambition, the time to finish writing a sentence because I loved the baby so much. I was a bleeding, leaking mammal, weeping in the produce section and fighting with my husband in the parking lot of Costco, but quietly so as not to wake the baby who had finally, finally fallen asleep in the back seat. I was a mother, and I was a beast.

Before I had a baby, I believed goodness was the highest goal. I had been good at school, good at my job. Surely, I would be a good mother, too. But when I had a baby, I found that for the first time, goodness was slippery, out of reach—impossible, even. This is a story about how I stopped being good.

. . .

This is also a story about the scientists and social scientists who made our myths about goodness. They're mostly men, their own children raised somewhere offstage, their examples as parents ones we mostly wouldn't want to follow. Some, like Dr. Spock, remain household names, while the fame of others, like the British psychoanalyst and psychologist John Bowlby and the Canadian American psychologist Mary Ainsworth, has faded a bit, even as their core ideas about what babies need and what it means to be a good mother haunt us still.

I began my research with psychologist Harry Harlow, whose studies, beginning in the 1950s, of monkey infants raised by cloth surrogate mothers seemed at first to provide a model of the perfect mother-baby pair, locked together by love. In his first presentation of that cloth mother research, which begins with the proclamation that "love is a wondrous state, deep, tender, and rewarding," Harlow sounds more like a poet than a scientist. (He acknowledges, in the sentence that follows, that love "is regarded by some as an improper topic for experimental research.") Harlow's research, which quickly spread beyond academic journals and dimly lit conference rooms and into newspapers, women's magazines, and television, captured the public imagination. In the first years of those studies, those baby monkeys and their constantly available, endlessly adoring cloth mothers seemed like the image of a good mother and her contented baby.

That image took on a particular urgency in the years following World War II, which had seen soldiers sent overseas, women participating in the war effort at home and abroad, and children attending state-supported childcare while their mothers worked. In the United Kingdom, the evidence of trauma from war was everywhere. Children who'd been evacuated from urban areas because of bombings struggled to readjust to life at home with their families; children who'd stayed in cities and had to shelter underground during the blitz earned the nickname "tube sleepers" after they lost the ability to sleep. European nations responded to wartime tragedies by eliminating the death penalty and expanding the social safety net. In the United States, the trauma of war was perhaps less visible, but families still struggled with a return to peacetime. Women's work outside the home had been essential to the war effort, and the government-subsidized childcare centers that had made that work possible were wildly popular with the mothers who used them. But urgency around getting men back into the jobs women had worked in their absence, combined with growing "Red Scare" concerns about what might happen to children cared for by someone other than their mother, meant the speedy closure of those daycares. Women were shuttled back into the home, and the growing suburbanization of the time period meant that mothers were increasingly isolated. Despite the revolutionary potential of that era, a reactionary social agenda won out. It sometimes feels like every generation of mothers from Betty Friedan and Adrienne Rich on has been learning anew that the story we've been sold about the magical power of a mother's love is largely a way to draft us into an enormous amount of unpaid and undervalued labor.

This book largely tells the story of ideals for white mothers. The "good mother" has always been imagined as white, straight, married, and middle class, and the postwar policies that helped create our modern image of the good mother at home with her children were aimed primarily at white families. Even policies that were racially neutral on their face, like the G.I. Bill's granting of educational benefits and VA home loans to veterans, disproportionately benefitted white male veterans. Black veterans faced significant difficulty in using the benefits to which they were entitled because of ongoing racial segregation; quotas in higher education; and redlining, racial covenants, and other policies that made it exceptionally difficult for Black families to buy homes. A nostalgic, ahistorical view of our past posits the fifties as a moment when America was "great," but the prosperity of that time was never equally shared. The narrow ideal of the good mother at home with her children, a breadwinning husband off at work, everyone happy and well-fed in a suburban home was only ever accessible to a portion of the white middle class for a sliver of the middle of the last century. Though this image has become encoded as the "traditional family," it's a historical mirage.

The cultural backlash of the eighties and nineties contributed to even more unrealistic expectations of mothers. As matricentric feminist scholar Andrea O'Reilly has observed, our standards for mothers have always increased at just the moment when women were making gains in public life, as in the rise of intensive mothering in the eighties and nineties when women were making inroads in the workforce, initiating divorce more often, and overtaking men in educational and professional accomplishments. In other words, our expectations of the "good mother" have tended to expand right as women began to take up space formerly granted to men. The high-intensity parenting practices of white middle-class families have come to be seen as the "best" way to raise kids, even for families without the social capital or wealth to parent that way. It's becoming ever harder to resist the individualistic, competitive way of parenting that insists that what kids need is constant supervision and stimulation, provided by a small army of tutors, coaches, and extracurriculars.

And this narrow, exclusionary vision of motherhood harms us all. Anyone who doesn't fit the impossible ideal—mothers who are fat, poor, queer, Black or Brown, people who've come to parenting through step-parenting or adoption, trans or non-binary people who've given birth but don't identify as moms—finds themselves the subject of additional scrutiny, cast beyond the halo of societal approval that adorns the "good mother." But even if your demographics line up with the ideal, you'll soon find that you're more likely to get words of encouragement (or criticism, depending on the day) than material support.

The landscape of reproductive healthcare following the Supreme Court's 2022 *Dobbs* decision, which overruled *Roe v. Wade*, has made the stakes of our ideals around mothers even clearer. People considering parenthood today now face, on one hand, wild-eyed rhetoric from politicians and pundits about self-ish young women choosing not to have children, and on the other, a web of laws making even planned pregnancies potentially lethal. As anthropologist Sarah Blaffer Hrdy has written, "Wherever women have both control over their reproductive opportunities and a chance to better themselves, women opt for well-being and economic security over having more children." The ability to choose when and how and with whom to have children has dramatically improved women's lives across the last two generations, and now we live in a time when those choices are severely constricted. As cases from Ohio to Texas have demonstrated, the full force of the law will always fall more heavily on pregnant people who are Black and Brown, but even being the blond married mother of two who's seeking an abortion after the diagnosis of a fatal fetal abnormality in a planned and wanted pregnancy won't save you. Exceptions for the life of the mother won't protect us if the powers that be believe a woman's life doesn't count for much.

The underlying problem is that the "good mother" isn't really a person. She's a subject of capitalism, charged with optimizing every aspect of her kids' childhood so she can produce good future workers and consumers. And this, too—the competitiveness and individualism that's baked into our image of the good mother sacrificing anything to get the best for her kids—is part of the trap. If we're indoors obsessing over whether our baby is meeting developmental milestones fast enough or which private preschool to select for our toddler, if we're memorizing scripts that promise to fix tantrums and googling lunchbox hacks, we're not out in our communities organizing for universal pre-K or free school lunches. The good mother thinks always of her own children first.

. . .

Why is the ideal of the good mother so seductive? At the time that I gave birth to my oldest child, I was a PhD student, well practiced in close reading, analytical thinking, and the questioning of received wisdom. The mythology of motherhood had seeped in so gradually I couldn't even notice it happening. I wrapped myself in an electric fence of my own expectations—feeling the sting of what felt like hundreds of mistakes I was making when my baby and I failed to immediately bond in a rosy cloud of maternal bliss.

The more I uncover about the ways that our ideals about motherhood came to be, the more I understand how inescapable these ideals have become, even—or maybe especially—for the savviest among us, those of us so used to overachieving that motherhood has become one more race to win. It was practically in the air of the liberal, slightly crunchy Madison of the early 2000s—where every coffee shop and park bench seemed dotted with good mothers who strolled, sipped, and chatted with peaceful babies cradled in soft fabric carriers against their chests. Today, it's on Instagram, where performing good motherhood has become a cottage industry. It's easy to dismiss this part of it as superficial—the good mother as an aesthetic—but scratch the surface of these images of organic cotton swaddles and ethically produced toys and discover the ways that our expectations of mothers are part of the network of power, economics, and morality that runs underneath society as a whole.

And that's the project of this book: to tell the history of our bad ideas about motherhood so we can begin to untangle ourselves from their grip. I believe that looking to the past helps us see the present more clearly. Nothing about our current culture around motherhood is natural or inevitable or unchangeable. When we understand how the structures and policies and culture that constrain us came to be, we can see our way into changing them.

. . .

In the earliest weeks of motherhood, when I'd been cracked open by birth and breastfeeding and sleep deprivation, I'd sometimes see women walking with older kids and have the crazed impulse to stop them and ask how they'd survived. I was so desperate to follow the right rules or learn the right trick. Some of the best advice I read during that time came from an essay I read on my phone while the baby napped in his stroller, about a woman who'd joined the circus and learned to eat fire. "The trick is there is no trick," she wrote. "How you eat fire is you eat fire." Caring for a newborn isn't quite like eating fire, but the point stands. There's no way to make it easy. But there are a lot of ways to make it harder: by worrying about what your friends or family or strangers on the internet will think about how you birth or feed or dress your baby, by spending hours scrolling social media for advice and expertise. By trying to do it all yourself.

I'll tell you how I survived: by asking for help and accepting it when it showed up. By being honest about how much I was struggling. By putting down the parenting advice manuals. By letting the baby cry it out so we could all finally get some sleep. By asking my husband to pitch in and letting him learn to parent in his own way. By giving up on the dream of being the perfect, self-sufficient, totally capable mother. By finally realizing that there's no way to actually be a good mother, and that that's not what my kids need anyway. My kids, like any kids, are their own weird, specific people, and what they need are parents who will love them and care for them as they are. They don't need a *good mother*. They just need love. (And, occasionally, to be told they really do have to put clean underwear on after the shower and for the bajillionth time to please go brush their teeth.)

In one way, Harlow was right about love. It is wondrous and rewarding. The love that I feel for my children has changed my life. But love isn't instant or automatic, and it doesn't make the labor of caring for an infant easy or instinctive. Our love, like any, took time to grow.

Before my first son was born, I believed both that I could read and research my way into motherhood and that mother-love would be instant and alchemical, transforming me into a sweeter, gentler, endlessly patient version of myself. I believed motherhood was both the most natural thing in the world and something that could be done correctly. I can see now what an impossible knot I'd made myself. I couldn't see it then. But I know now that we can set aside our bad ideas and imagine something new.

1

A Perfect Monkey Mother

After the baby was born, we'd stayed in the hospital as long as they'd let us, eating tasteless food and relying on the nurses for help with changing diapers and a first bath. In the first picture we shared of him online, when he was only a few hours old, the baby was wrapped tight in a hospital swaddle, his bright blue eyes staring at me with the deep wisdom of a newborn. We named him Penn, after the street in Pittsburgh where my husband lived when we first fell in love, and after William Penn and the entire state of Pennsylvania, which still felt then more like home than any of the other places we'd lived in our time together. That first night in the hospital, he woke once in the clear-sided bassinet beside me. I woke easily and lifted him, patting his little diapered butt until he fell back asleep. When the lactation specialist visited during our last morning in the hospital, she said we were doing great. "I think you'll get through this just fine," she assured me.

And then it was time to go home. I walked down the windowed hallway of the hospital unencumbered as my husband, Smith, carried the baby in his car seat, my duffel tossed across his shoulder. The maternity shirt I'd worn on our arrival sagged a little now. I was one person again. The baby blinked and wiggled in the car seat. I'd bought him a special "going-home" outfit—a cream-colored set with a onesie, pants, and hat, made of organic cotton with tiny ribs—but the baby was so delicate, I couldn't bring myself to pull the onesie over his floppy head and down over the bandaged stub of his umbilical cord. I'd dressed him instead in a hand-me-down from one of my sisters, a green-and-white-striped onesie that snapped across the belly.

On our first afternoon home from the hospital, Smith went out to the Jenny Street Market, the little grocer on our side of town that only took cash and sold local brats at their butcher counter, and I found myself alone with the baby. I didn't know what to do. He didn't seem to need anything from me, though I didn't know yet what babies needed, not really. I sat on the couch and stared at the baby, wriggling in the swing, as he blinked back at me.

And then, that first night home, the baby howled. Our mild, wide-eyed baby roared from inside his tiny toothless mouth. I laid him down on the bedspread and wrapped the muslin swaddle tight around him as he kicked and flailed. I patted his back and walked with him, then handed him over to Smith when nothing I tried made a difference. I sat on the bed as he rocked and shushed the swaddled baby, lightly jiggling him the way the Happiest Baby on the Block video from our labor and delivery class had shown. We were doing everything right, and the baby kept on screaming. The ceiling fan whirled above us. The globes of the baby's cheeks turned pink, then red. The tufts of hair on his new head spiked up. It was 10:00 P.M., then it was 11:00, then it was past midnight and the baby was still howling. Time split open.

I sat with the baby in bed and nursed him, over and over. Nothing helped. I unlatched my nursing tank and lifted the baby to my breast one more time and Smith snapped, "You just did that. I don't think it's going to help."

I took the baby into my husband's office, where I shushed and rocked him for hours. I'd heard babies cry before, at restaurants and parks, had registered the sound as a nuisance but not a catastrophe. This sound was new. It was an emergency inside my entire body. I believed that if we could make it to morning, something would have to change. I'd call everyone I could think of and someone would help.

Sometime before dawn the baby finally dropped off and I laid him down carefully on the flat surface of the Pack'n Play we'd set up beside our bed. I lay down beside him, exhausted but wired. I must have slept, too, eventually, and my husband and I woke when the morning light came pouring through the bathroom window across the hall and directly into our eyes.

. . .

I called the doctor's office that morning as soon as they opened. As I got transferred from one receptionist to another, my voice grew thick, and by the time I'd gotten connected to the lactation specialist's scheduler, I could barely say my own name through sobs. "Can you come in at 11:15?" she asked. "Can you hold on until then?"

We held on, and while we waited in the lobby for our appointment, the receptionist peeked into the car seat where the baby was sleeping, of course, like an angel and not like a baby who'd screamed so hard and long in the middle of the night that he had sweated right through the muslin swaddle that was supposed to soothe him. She smiled and said, "Oh, enjoy it. They're only that little such a short while." I smiled back at her and did not say, *That is the kind of thing people say when they have not lived with a newborn for a long, long time.*

Inside the lactation specialist's office, I lifted my shirt and unhooked the nursing tank, and the lactation specialist and her nurse both took a startled step back. I'd been told that early nursing could hurt, but apparently it wasn't normal for nipples to be raw and cracked. I'd caused this injury, they explained, by nursing the baby with a bad latch, so that instead of getting milk, the baby sucked the skin raw. No one had told me—not the lactation specialist who taught the breastfeeding class I'd obediently taken while pregnant, not the nurses or lactation specialists at the hospital—that, a few days after birth, when we were all supposed to be settling in happily at home, my milk would come in in a sudden rush, my breasts so engorged that my nipples would look like a crumb on the dinner plate of my areola, the whole thing so big and flat that there was no way the baby could latch. Or maybe they did tell me that, and I'd been too exhausted and incredulous to take it in.

The lactation specialist taught me how to manually express a bit of milk, squirting carefully into a small plastic cup, so that, one at a time, each breast would disengorge itself, a recognizable nipple emerging from the milk-filled mass, and the baby could latch. She demonstrated the positions—the football hold and the cradle hold—that we'd practiced with dolls at breastfeeding class. She showed us how to pat the baby with damp paper towels to keep him cold and awake enough to nurse. He'd just been getting the smallest amount of milk, she said, enough to let him fall asleep briefly, but not enough to really fill him and let him get a good rest. She taught me to time how long I nursed on each side—ten minutes in the cradle hold on the right, then ten on the left; ten minutes in the football hold on the right, then ten on the left—so that I'd feed the baby a total of forty minutes before trying to get him back to sleep.

That day, in her office, all four of us worked together to feed the baby, weighing him after he nursed on each side so we were sure he'd gotten enough milk. He fell asleep in his car seat, slept the whole way home, and took a good long nap, undisturbed even after we carried him inside and left him sleeping in his car seat on the dining room floor.

• • •

Left to our own devices back at home, nothing worked quite so easily. It took two sets of adult hands to get a decent latch for nursing. My steady, capable husband, who had replaced all the lead pipes in our old house with shiny new copper, who had knelt beside me and calmed me through the worst parts of a long labor, now used those hands to hold the baby's hands away from his face while I used one hand to compress my breast, turning the nipple into a projectile, and the other to shove the baby's open, wailing mouth toward my chest. I'd thought of nursing as my job—I was the one with the boobs, after all—and I hated needing help, hated handling my own breasts in such a functional way in front of my husband. I felt like livestock.

I timed the nursing on my phone, watching the seconds tick away. Women on the internet and at the nursing classes had described letdown, the feeling when the milk starts to flow after the baby's latched. For some it felt like a rush, and some said it hurt, like a sharp sting. But either way, it was proof that your body responded to the baby like it should. I never felt letdown like that, but after a time, I could see that it was working: the flange of the baby's lips, wide around my nipple; the *click, click* of his swallows as milk went down his throat.

But even with a good latch and a full belly, the baby screamed after nursing. Everyone said a swaddle was the best thing to soothe a baby, but when we wrapped him up, he tightened all the muscles of his infant core to arch back and howl. I'd start trying to nurse him down between ten or eleven, and some nights we'd be up until one or later while he cried. Nothing worked. The baby cried until eventually, after hours, he gave up.

He slept and woke up screaming, and each time he woke I felt despair. The baby was beautiful, his dark blue eyes deep and wise. In the daytime, he rested peacefully in his swing, his fingers tented above his belly. The diaper was fastened loosely because the stub of his umbilical cord was still attached. And at night, he screamed like he knew the truth about me. At night, I knew it, too: the baby was perfect, and I was bad.

The love I'd felt for the baby on his birth was immediate and biological, just as I'd expected. But that love didn't seem to help.

Uncovering the Nature of Love

Across town, on the University of Wisconsin campus, the primate laboratory still carried the name of Harry Harlow, a psychologist who'd devoted his career to the study of maternal love. I'd first learned about Harlow's work early in grad school, when I'd heard the story that Harlow's lab had originally been in the basement of the brutalist concrete building where I took my classes. (Alas, this turns out to be not quite true; while the psychology department had been on the same site as our building, Harlow's actual lab was across campus. But the image—those baby monkeys, wracked by love—had a certain romantic appeal that no doubt contributed to the story's circulation among poets and aspiring English PhDs.) Newborn monkeys were raised in long rows of cages in Harlow's lab. In the experiment that would make him famous, each cage was equipped with two "mothers," one a bare wire cylinder and the other a wire cylinder wrapped in terrycloth and warmed by a light bulb. The cloth mother dispensed milk in some cages, and in others, the wire mother fed the baby. No matter which mother fed them, the baby monkeys clung to their cloth mother, gripping her warm form for as many as seventeen to eighteen hours a day. As I sat in graduate seminar after graduate seminar in the seventh-floor classroom overlooking Lake Mendota, I'd pictured those monkeys in the basement far below me, clinging to their cloth mothers. The babies were so besotted with those cloth mothers, I'd read, that even when Harlow devised an experiment he called the "Evil Mother," in which the cloth mother occasionally sprouted spikes that poked the babies, the babies sprang away from the spikes but immediately returned to the mother who'd attacked them.

Before I was a mother, I thought about the babies, their pitiful enormous faces, their plaintive almost-human hands gripping cloth. That initial interest was aesthetic: as a poet, I was obsessed with the image of those baby monkeys, so nearly human, so eager for love. That image glowed with resonance, and I scrawled lines about it in my notebooks.

After my baby was born, I thought about the cloth mothers. The babies clung to them and were, Harlow wrote, completely satisfied by their warm cloth-wrapped bodies. But my baby was anything but satisfied with me. He refused to be soothed, and at night, that image of the cloth monkey mother and the baby who loved her haunted me.

In the nighttime, I rocked and patted and shushed the baby in the gray light of the nursery. And in the daytime, I began a research project. I found Harlow's papers in the library databases, watched black-and-white video of him walking corridors of cages that held monkeys and their substitute mothers. If Harlow had discovered what made a mother good, and if he'd done it on the same campus where I studied, I wanted to learn it, too.

But when I began reading Harlow's work, I found that there was far more to the story than that frozen image of the adoring baby. The still frame came to life and drew me in. I read Harlow's studies and his popular work and the biographies that showed his personal struggles alongside his professional rise and fall. What I uncovered—about Harlow and his monkeys and how those studies have resonated through psychology and popular culture—would prove to be far more complicated than I'd ever guessed.

From Learning to Love

Harlow hadn't set out to study monkeys, or mothers, or love. He'd come to Wisconsin in 1930 fresh from a PhD at Stanford, where he'd had rats as research subjects in complicated studies of learning. Rats were the gold standard for comparative psychologists at the time—readily available, easy to breed, responsive to any stimulus a scientist might want to measure. In those labs, a new batch of rats ran each maze, ensuring that the results stayed pure and weren't influenced by anything the rats had learned through previous experiments. Later, after he'd moved into primate research, Harlow described the ideal outcome for a standard psychology experiment of this time: "The controls are perfect, the results are important, and the rats are dead." This kind of animal research, where results could be measured and graphed and replicated, was an essential element of psychology's efforts at proving its worth. It wasn't just Dr. Freud and couches and dream analysis; it was a rigorous empirical science. Psychology might be the study of the mysterious human mind, but as an emerging discipline, it was working to prove its status as a science through graphs and charts and quantitative, replicable results.

Harlow had been promised a rat laboratory when he was hired as an assistant professor at Wisconsin, but when he arrived in Madison, he was told that the lab had been torn down and there were no plans to replace it. He tried a variety of other approaches—the attic rooms of one building, which turned murderously hot in summer; a basement space in Bascom Hall, where the rat smells floated up into the Dean of Men's office; the basement of a fraternity house, where he and his students experimented with conditioning cats until one leaped up and ran right out an open window. For a time, he experimented with frogs before declaring to a lecture hall full of undergrads that they were the dumbest of all the animals, too stupid to even be conditioned through electric shock.

The solution, and the turn to primate research, came over the bridge table at a dinner party, when a guest offered a suggestion: "Why not go to the Vilas Park Zoo and do research on the monkeys there?" Writing later about this career-shaping moment, Harlow noted that the guest, Mrs. Hemnon, was "the chairman's wife," but perhaps more importantly, she was a Vilas, the same family who'd granted the land for the zoo and for whom the adjacent neighborhood is named. The Henry Vilas Zoo had completed work on its primate house just one year before Harlow moved to Madison, and when he and his students arrived at the zoo, they found a pair of orangutans, Maggie and Jiggs, and a baboon named Tommy, who proved to be excellent initial subjects.

Though Harlow would do research in the zoo for only two years before establishing his first primate lab in a makeshift concrete building on what he called "the wrong side of the Milwaukee railroad tracks," his experience with the primates there forever changed his research trajectory from learning to love. Harlow observed the zoo director, Fred Winkelman, leading the orangutan Maggie around the zoo's walkways while holding her hand. The baboon, Tommy, had a short temper, tearing up test objects and smashing the test tray against the bars of his cage when he made mistakes. Yet Tommy developed a marked preference for one research assistant, Betty. When Betty visited, she fed Tommy grapes and peanuts. She let him groom her arms. And when she tested him, he'd persist through mistakes. Seeing these relationships firsthand between primates and humans led Harlow to observe that "the monkeys were so very, very much like people." Rats could be used to prove or disprove a narrow hypothesis about conditioning or learning, perhaps. But monkeys seemed to offer insight into human behavior and relationships. Writing about this early research, Harlow insisted, "These are not just monkey stories. They are human-interest stories."

Despite his rigorous training as a scientist, focused only on observable facts, something about monkeys led Harlow in a more fanciful direction. And it's easy to see how Harlow, spending day after day learning the particular personalities of those primates, came to leap so quickly from monkeys to human mothers. Maggie, Jiggs, and Tommy weren't human, but they were far closer to humans than the rats he'd spent his doctoral research studying.

Even today, we often look to animals to try to figure out how things might be in nature, how perhaps they *should* be, were it not for humans and their pesky feelings and evolving culture. We're especially quick to look to animals as evidence of what should be when we're talking about women and motherhood. It comes up all the time with breastfeeding, which is so often presented as the most natural thing in the world. Dogs and cows and rats do it, after all, and they don't have lactation consultants to help.

I'd wanted mothering to be simple and natural, too. I'd wanted to be guided by maternal instinct out of my own buzzing brain and back into my primate body that would show me how to care for my baby without minding or thinking of anything else. But mothering is never that simple. Not for human mothers, and not, it turns out, for monkey mothers, either.

· · ·

In the early 1950s, after his stint at the zoo and a few years in a small, cobbled-together primate lab, Harlow's lab moved into an abandoned cheese factory, where his famous experiments on mothers and babies began. With more space in the new lab, Harlow and his researchers decided to breed their own colony of monkeys, rather than relying on animals imported from India, which often arrived sick and starved from the journey. To reduce the risk of infection, they raised this first generation of babies in cages separate from their mothers and from all other monkeys, but quickly found that these apparently healthy monkeys were far from normal. They wouldn't socialize and wouldn't breed, but sat in their cages and stared at each other. It seemed these monkeys needed something more than food and hygienic living conditions to become functional adults. These challenges with infant monkeys led Harlow to turn his attention toward mothers and babies.

The solution came to Harlow all at once, and the cloth mother, he wrote later, was "born in a Boeing stratocruiser high over Detroit." On that flight, Harlow explained, "as I turned to look out the window, I suddenly had a vision of the cloth surrogate mother sitting beside me in her bold and barren splendor." When Harlow got home to Madison, he immediately set to work recruiting grad students to help build his surrogate mother and test its effect on the baby monkeys.

The cloth mother was simple in form: nothing more than a wire cylinder wrapped in terrycloth and warmed. But Harlow believed he'd made a perfect monkey mother—"soft, warm, and tender, a mother with infinite patience, a mother available twenty-four hours a day, a mother that never scolded her infant and never struck or bit her baby in anger"—and the experimental results seemed to prove him right. All those hours the baby monkeys spent clinging to their cloth mothers seemed, in those initial experiments, like proof that constant contact comfort was a caregiver's most essential responsibility. As Harlow's research was picked up by other scientists and circulated in newspapers and women's magazines and on TV, that constantly available, totally adoring cloth mother became a model for the ideal human mother, too.

I'd imagined myself as a kind of cloth mother, able to become soft and warm and yielding for the baby. All the good mothers who surrounded me in Madison seemed like cloth mothers, too, their babies dressed in organic cotton and cloth diapers, cradled in fabric wraps, shielded from the sun by the printed muslin swaddles that got softer with each wash. The other new mothers I knew posted pictures of their peaceful sleeping babies with captions describing the hours they lost to staring at their faces while they napped. But when I rocked the baby to sleep, my mind buzzed with all the other things I wanted to be doing.

In 1958, Harlow was elected the president of the American Psychological Association, and when he gave the president's address at that year's conference, he seized the opportunity to share his cloth mother research in a talk he called "The Nature of Love." Harlow's talk was peppered with puns and included a twenty-minute film of the monkeys and their cloth mothers. It was held in the ballroom on the Saturday evening of the conference, after he led the Annual Report to the Members of the APA Forum, which coincided with the Reception for Wives of APA Members, and before the All APA Dance. There was a break for dinner, and I imagine all of those psychologists, and perhaps some of their wives, returning to the ballroom, full of flavorless conference food, sitting in rows of folding chairs and filling the air with smoke as Harlow spoke. In that talk, Harlow told the story of a woman who approached him after he had given a speech, her face, in his retelling, "brightened with sudden insight." "Now I know what's wrong with me," she told him. "I'm just a wire mother." (Harlow, in the casual misogyny he was often willing to play for jokes, followed his recounting of that heartrending confession with a joke: "Perhaps she was lucky. She might have been a wire wife.")

And what about me? If I loved the baby, but not to the exclusion of everything else in my life, not at the cost of everything I'd been and done before his birth, what kind of a mother did that make me? Was I a wire mother, capable of dispensing milk but not love?

Today, Harlow's conclusions can feel obvious: of course a

baby needs not only food but also love to thrive. At the time, however, Harlow's work was groundbreaking. Just a generation before, experts had warned parents against cuddling or coddling their babies. Psychologist John B. Watson intoned, in his popular parenting book from 1928, *Psychological Care of Infant and Child*, that "mother-love is a dangerous instrument." You must never kiss your child, Watson warned, though he did allow that parents might grant their child "a pat on the head if they have made an extraordinary job of a difficult task." We know now, of course, that a baby can't be spoiled by love. But the parents of Harlow's time had grown up in an era when all the experts advised rigid schedules for feeding and sleeping, when credible scientists regarded babies as passive lumps. The idea that a newborn might actually need the love that Watson had warned against was a sea change in how we think about children and caregiving. Harlow's work was crucial in shaping what we now think of as simply common sense.

Harlow faced critics from within his own discipline, including those who objected to his use of the word "love" when talking about monkeys and mother surrogates, instead of the disciplinary jargon about "drive reduction" and "conditioned response" any respectable psychologist would use. When one critic suggested that what Harlow was really measuring was not love but merely the infant's proximity to its cloth mother, Harlow was quick with a retort, snapping that "perhaps all you've known in life is proximity. I thank God I've known more." Earlier psychologists had characterized a child's connection to their mother as merely "cupboard love," not a genuine feeling but simply the conditioned response to being fed, but Harlow's research began to point the way toward thinking about this earliest relationship as love. Observing the infant monkeys and their cloth mothers, he remarked on their "togetherness." For Harlow, love was observable and quantifiable, but it was also fluid, a bit mystical, something that grew between mother and baby over time.

And even more persuasive than the quantitative data were the images. When you saw the wide-eyed babies of Harlow's experiments, with their long, nearly-human hands clinging to the mother who comforted them, it just looked like love. In a photograph accompanying a 1959 *Scientific American* article by Harlow, a baby monkey presses her whole body along the length of the cloth mother, arms wrapped around each side of her cylindrical form. The cloth mother's faces were deliberately ugly, their eyes made of red bicycle reflectors, their mouths half-moons of green plastic. And still, the baby seems to be gazing into her mother's eyes. Her face is pressed against the black-painted maple button that forms her nose. Looking at the photo, it's easy to see why Harlow believed he'd discovered love.

"It's Mother Who Counts"

It turns out I wasn't the only one smitten by Harlow's perfect monkey mothers and their adoring babies. The British psychiatrist and psychoanalyst John Bowlby saw in Harlow's monkey studies hard proof of the theory he was then developing: that mother and baby were designed, by both nature and evolution, to be a perfect pair. Bowlby's work, known today as attachment theory, argues that what a baby needs most is the constant, uninterrupted devotion of a single primary caregiver, ideally the biological mother—and that any interruption to this bond puts the child's long-term physical and emotional well-being in dire risk. To this way of thinking, a mother who's continually available, who's responsive to her child's every need and whim, is just doing what she's been designed by nature to do. And a mother who falls short of this high bar puts her child's entire future in danger.

(It might be a little rude to psychoanalyze a psychoanalyst, but I can't help but point out that Bowlby's lifelong obsession with mothers may have an origin in his personal life. Bowlby grew up in the kind of prewar, upper-crust English family—I always picture *Downton Abbey*—that hired teams of nannies to raise their children, who were brought down from the nursery for one hour each afternoon to see their mother. As a small child, Bowlby had been cared for largely by his nanny Minnie, and when she left the family, then-four-year-old Bowlby was as devastated as if he'd lost a parent. Some men really will invent an entire academic discipline instead of going to therapy.)

Bowlby had been writing about the perils of inadequate mothers since the beginning of his career, when he worked as a psychiatrist to "delinquent" children at the London Child Guidance Clinic. He drew on this clinical work in his 1944 study, "Forty-Four Juvenile Thieves," which analyzed the cases of forty-four children referred to the London Child Guidance Clinic for stealing, plus a control group of forty-four children who'd been deemed "unstable or neurotic" but not "thieves." In his analysis, Bowlby focused only on what he called "the personal environment of the child," by which he meant the mother. He did not gather information about the father or the extended family, and he did not take into account anything about the children's housing conditions, school attendance, or family income. Instead, he identified a subgroup of children who had been separated from their mothers and concluded that it was the mother's absence, whether caused by the mother's death, foster care, or the child's hospitalization, that had led the children to their misbehavior. (It seems obvious, but I'll say it anyway: certainly a portion of those petty thefts, which Bowlby took as evidence of deficient mental health, would be better explained by poverty than maternal absence. Since Bowlby didn't collect data on the children's socioeconomic status, he couldn't take that into account, and we can't, either.) Bowlby, who admitted to having "a rather one-track, one-problem mind," determined that mothers were the root cause of all of children's problems at the very beginning of his career, and he would stick to that explanation for the rest of his life.

Following World War II, as psychologists, policymakers, and politicians worried about the psychological impact of the war, which had left an estimated thirteen million orphans across Europe and countless more children homeless and traumatized, Bowlby was enlisted by the World Health Organization to investigate the mental health of homeless children. He again found, remarkably, that it was mothers who were to blame when children suffered. His report on the matter, published by the WHO in 1951 as *Maternal Care and Mental Health*, came to a dramatic conclusion: the most important factor in a child's mental health was the constant care and devotion of their mother.

Let's pause for a moment here and note how wild it is that Bowlby was charged with studying the well-being of homeless children following a global war—and came back with a report arguing that the primary problem those children faced was inadequate maternal care. Many of those mothers were working, as their government had urged, to support the war effort, while trying to feed their families on rations and whatever they might grow in a victory garden; many had sent their children to the countryside, also at their government's urging, to keep them safe; surely all of those mothers were dealing with their own trauma following what would have been for many of them the second world war of their lifetime. None of that is enough, it turns out, to absolve you from accusations of being a bad mom.

Though these kinds of studies are usually read only by experts and quickly consigned to dusty archives, Bowlby's work hit the culture at the right moment and caught fire. The press loved his ideas, and his work was discussed in newspapers from South Africa to Italy. Reporting on Bowlby's work in 1952, the *Daily Mail* asked "What Makes a Child Grow Up 'Good' or 'Bad'?" and answered "It's Mother Who Counts." The article went on to explain that "mother-love is to the budding personality what sunshine is to a flower; it yields the vitamins vital to mental health." In Bowlby's day, psychologists and the general public alike were largely interested in mental health as a shorthand for producing children and young adults who would avoid theft and antisocial behavior. Rather than worrying about depression and anxiety, in other words, they were more interested in ensuring that the next generation of workers would marry, raise children, and generally not question the status quo. Bowlby's report was reprinted five times between 1951 and 1952, and a condensed version, published in 1953 as a paperback titled *Child Care and the Growth of Love*, sold more than 400,000 copies in its English edition and was translated into more than fourteen languages.

Certainly one cause of Bowlby's popularity was his willingness, despite the fact that he'd been studying homeless children, to apply his theories to all children. In perhaps the most-quoted phrase of the whole report, Bowlby argued that what an infant and young child most needed was "a warm, intimate, and continuous relationship with his mother." When he listed the evils that would contribute to a disastrous breakdown in the home, Bowlby placed "war, famine, death of a parent, desertion, imprisonment" right alongside—truly, in the same bulleted list—"full-time employment of the mother."

If Bowlby's attachment theory, with its emphasis on the constant care of a totally adoring mother, a woman with no thoughts or ambitions beyond her home and children, sounds like a caricature of a fifties housewife, there's good reason for that. Though Bowlby worked hard throughout his career to cast his theory as objective science, it's very much a product of the particular postwar soup of anxieties about gender, family life, and the economy that also gave rise to McCarthyism, color television, the polio vaccine, and, ironically, the Barbie doll. Attachment theory presented itself as science, but it's inextricable from the concerns of its day. Across Europe and the United States, huge numbers of women had worked as part of the war effort—more than one and a half million mothers of young children in the US alone—and the state-run childcare that had made this possible was wildly popular. But with veterans returning home from war, politicians and public thinkers were worried about getting men back to work and women back home to care for children. Attachment theory gave them convenient cover to answer: sorry, ladies, science says you have to stay home.

When Bowlby came up against criticisms, particularly from American psychologists, he turned to the animal world to bolster his emerging theory. He became enamored first with Konrad Lorenz, an Austrian zoologist who'd garnered attention for his studies of birds and imprinting, the process by which a bird fixes on the first figure it sees after hatching. Lorenz entered pop culture in America when he was featured in a 1955 *Life* magazine article, photographed surrounded by his goslings, under the headline "An Adopted Mother Goose." The fact that he'd been a member of the Nazi party and had worked as a psychiatrist in the German Army during the war is left out of this sweet public image. The historical record is uncertain on the precise nature of Lorenz's work as an assistant to a notorious "race psychologist" during the war, but it still seems like a pretty good idea to not take parenting advice shaped by a literal Nazi.

Though Lorenz studied geese and ducks and jackdaws, he insisted that mothering behavior in both birds and women was biological and automatic rather than learned. For Lorenz, a mother didn't really have, or even need, a mind. Instead, Lorenz believed that pregnancy and birth kicked off the maternal instincts that had been lying in wait all along. Bowlby enthusiastically took up Lorenz's ideas about maternal instincts in his arguments about the enormous power of a mother's love.

When Bowlby learned of Harlow's cloth mother studies during a sabbatical year he spent at Stanford, it must have felt like a dream: a well-respected psychologist doing research that seemed like empirical, unshakable proof of what he'd believed all along about mothers and babies. Bowlby wrote to Harlow in August 1957, introducing himself and offering to mail a copy of the paper he was then developing. He asked if Harlow might send him any of his own research, either published papers or drafts. Harlow replied with enthusiasm just a few days later, noting that Bowlby's work was "closely akin to a research program that I am developing on maternal responses in monkeys." That initial correspondence sparked a decades-long professional collaboration. "It is an understatement to add that we have research interests in common," Harlow wrote to Bowlby in January 1958. In April of that year, Bowlby saw Harlow give a talk at a conference in Monterey, and in June, he finally made it to Madison for the much-anticipated visit to see Harlow's monkeys and their mothers.

Across that first year of correspondence, both men were homing in on the work that would make them famous. By the time he received Bowlby's first letter, Harlow's colony of rhesus monkeys, the first self-sustaining colony of monkeys in the United States, was flourishing, and he was beginning to share the results from his cloth mother studies with colleagues at conferences. In his first letter to Bowlby, Harlow described the talk he was preparing for his address at the American Psychological Association. That talk, "The Nature of Love," and the adapted version of it published later in *Scientific American* for a general audience, would propel him to national and international attention. The work Bowlby shared with Harlow was a draft of "The Nature of the Child's Tie to His Mother," which would define the key principles of attachment theory. In those landmark papers, each man cited the other. Their ideas, in those early years, seemed so perfectly in sync. Bowlby began with psychoanalysis and grounded those ideas with observational studies of children in clinics and orphanages. Harlow began with the rigor of experimental science and used his meticulous records to provide evidence of the power of a mother's love. Each man presented his argument in the flagship publication of his field, and each paper pushed up against the boundaries of its home discipline. For a time, each man's research seemed to shore up the other's.

Even a Man Might Be a Mother

Even as Harlow and his cloth mothers garnered attention from journalists and scientists alike, some important findings from those early studies were shuttled to the side in favor of that idealized image of the adoring baby and his devoted mother.

Because the babies loved the mothers who comforted them,

rather than the ones who fed them, Harlow concluded that nursing itself didn't create the mother-baby bond. Though his scientific language is clunky—"lactation is a variable of negligible importance"—the message still feels radical. Harlow concluded that the real purpose of nursing is that it ensures "frequent and intimate bodily contact of the infant with the mother." In other words: there's no magic in the act of breastfeeding that produces or transmits love. If you're holding your baby and keeping them fed, that's how love begins to grow. Recent studies in neuroscience have borne this out, showing that caregiving itself sets off a whole host of neurobiological changes. When researchers studied the brains of gay dads and foster parents, they found a dosage effect, meaning that the more time those parents spent caring for their babies, the more their brains were changed by that care. There's nothing magic about a specific gender or genetic relationship to a child; what counts is the care.

Perhaps even more radically, Harlow argued for a practical application of his research inside American homes: if it was not nursing but love, in the form of contact comfort, that made a healthy infant, men could do it just as well as women. In his words, "the American male is physically endowed with all the really essential equipment to compete with the American female on equal terms in one essential activity: the rearing of infants." One newspaper reporter, commenting on Harlow's work, put it more simply: "anyone can be a mother."

Most reporters, however, focused instead on the image of the baby and the cloth mother and skipped right over these more controversial applications of the work, which might have put babies and bottles in more men's arms. And Harlow was not, as his own children grew, applying this lesson to his own life. He knew he had the equipment to care for his children, but he preferred long hours in the lab to life at home. Counter to the image of the good mother at home with her child, this final, forgotten finding from Harlow's early research suggested that anyone with warm arms and a bottle could care for a child.

This is what I find most hopeful about Harlow and his monkeys: the idea that love isn't necessarily instant or automatic. It's not immediately produced by pregnancy or birth or nursing. At first, loving a baby is mostly just labor. Any man or monkey or imperfect mother might do.

If I'd known the fuller story of Harlow's monkeys and their cloth mothers in my first weeks of motherhood, I might have been able to be gentler with myself. I wish that I could travel back now and sit in the nighttime nursery beside that sore and weepy new mother version of myself, crying and cradling a crying baby, alone together in the dark. If I could, I'd lean over and tell her: *You're trying so hard. You're already doing great.*

The longer story of Harlow's research and those cloth mother–raised monkeys would prove more complicated, but in those early years, Harlow was still trying to discover what love was, exactly. He was more willing than most scientists of his generation to talk about love, but he still wanted to observe and measure it. Where did it come from? Was love an instinct, switched on at birth, or was the desire to care stitched somehow into the genes? When Harlow appeared on television, in the 1959 premiere of the CBS TV show *Conquest*, hosted by the former war correspondent Charles Collingwood, these questions were on center stage. The journalist and the scientist watched together as a baby monkey rocked against his cloth mother to soothe himself. Collingwood then asked a question that Harlow would pursue through the rest of his career: "But is this really love?"

. . .

That first summer of my first baby's life, a few miles and fifty years away from Harlow's lab, I was struggling with that same question. That first night at home, and all the wailing that followed it, shook the calm assurance I'd had in those peaceful first three days in the hospital. When I couldn't soothe the baby, when nursing wouldn't calm him, when he didn't respond to my voice or my touch, I took that to mean there was something deeply wrong with me. I'd wanted to be able to love and care for the baby basically on my own, to be the person he knew and loved above all, who was best able to anticipate and seamlessly meet his needs. And when I couldn't—when I needed help from my husband, from one lactation specialist and then another—I was angry at needing help, and resentful of everyone who tried to help me.

I can see now that I'd learned the wrong lesson. My problem wasn't that I couldn't care for the baby all on my own. It's that I was trying to.

Midcentury Science Reaches into the New Millennium

After two weeks of paternity leave, Smith was back to work, but since he worked from home, we were all still home all day together. I'd assumed I would take care of the baby while he worked, until I went back to campus in the fall and we figured out piecemeal childcare. But caring for the baby was both harder and more all-consuming than I'd imagined, so while Smith signed on to the work computer in his home office, I walked the house crying and coming apart at the seams. One day, I'd finally gotten the baby down for a nap and he was sleeping, swaddled, against my shoulder. I stood in the doorway of Smith's office, crying, and waited for him to see me. When he finally looked up from his monitor, I sobbed, "I'm sorry. I'm sorry I'm not doing a better job. I'm sorry I'm letting you down."

"What?" he responded, genuinely confused. "Look at that beautiful baby. We're doing great."

I couldn't see what he was seeing. I was trying so hard to be a *good mother* I couldn't see our actual child.

Neither of us knew anything about babies before Penn was born. But I was the one who carried the baby; I was his mother. I'd expected to be transformed. I'd absorbed such deep messages about the magic of motherhood, how once the baby was born, my deep love for him would make all the sleepless nights worth it, how my maternal instincts would teach me how to care for him. That was what I understood a good mother to be: someone who's capable, because of biology and love, of caring for the baby totally on her own. And that was what I saw all around me, those years in Madison, all those good mothers, who certainly would have identified as feminists, and yet, as soon as they had babies, they were in a world of women. I watched them, walking in the farmers market, sitting at the café next door to Happy Bambino with their tea and their babies sleeping in slings. Where were *their* husbands? I didn't once wonder. The mother and her baby made a complete world all their own.

This is the way attachment theory is still with us. Though I didn't know the name John Bowlby when I first became a mother, his ideas were in the air all around me: the smart, am-bitious women I'd worked with in my twenties, who'd left their careers when they had children because they wanted to be really present for all those early moments; the focus on bonding in the earliest weeks of a child's life as a time to forge a connection that would last a lifetime; the belief that mothers had special, innate knowledge of their children's moods and needs. Attachment theory has had a powerful influence on what we think makes a good mother, and because it's so pervasive, that influence has been nearly subterranean. Of course a child does best with the devoted care of his mother, of course the first years set a child on a trajectory that will be all but impossible to alter later. Once those ideas have taken root, they're hard to even name, much less resist.

Bowlby certainly didn't invent unrealistic expectations for mothers. Each era has had its own impossible ideal. You could think of the Victorian-era image of the Angel in the House, or the Revolutionary War–era Republican Mother, whose education and intellect were valued only because they allowed her to shape the character of the next generation of citizens. Those ideals, of course, only held for white women; in the same era, Black and Brown women were subject to forced sterilization, and enslaved women had long had their children stolen from them. For Bowlby and others, it was really only white middle-class mothers who were worth researching and improving.

Bowlby's particular genius was to draw together research from multiple fields, including the natural sciences, which held a higher status than his home field of psychology, and hand-pick the pieces that best supported his ideas. Bowlby and Harlow both excelled at using the popular press to circulate their ideas, and journalists were eager to promote the science that so nicely aligned with the cultural imperatives of the day. Together, Bowlby and Harlow took ideas about motherhood that had long been ambient in the culture and encased them in the durable shell of science.

And, of course, if it's true that a child's physical and psychological health, their present and future well-being, all depend on the mother's total devotion, if it's true that "the future of a child's mind is determined by her mother's heart," as one scholar characterized Bowlby's work, then it makes a certain sense to accept that becoming a mother means setting aside all your own interests and needs. With the approach of the Cold War, the private work of mothers took on public stakes: it wasn't just about raising healthy individual children, but about ensuring a future generation that could fight Communism and win the space race. No sacrifice could be too small in safeguarding the future of your child and the nation.

Attachment theory made the consequences of mothers' labor clear. Here, it seemed, was hard proof that a mother's constant care for her child was her valuable contribution to her family and her country. Anything less than total devotion would have devastating repercussions. That harm would reverberate not only through that child's life but would spiral outward to the entire community.

But what if the line from an endlessly adoring mother to a healthy child isn't so certain? What if all that science is, in fact, much shakier than we've been led to believe?

2

Overly Attached

When the baby was three weeks old, we went to a going-away party for a friend. It was at Old Sugar, a bar we'd gone to for years, where we'd gathered for birthday parties and an engagement party for friends and even once or twice for a department happy hour during the holidays. The baby had fallen asleep in the car ride over, and I set his car seat gently down on one of the high-top tables, made from an old distillery barrel. (One benefit of having babies in Wisconsin is that it's entirely normal to take them to the bar.) Smith walked toward the counter to place our orders.

I stood a moment, slightly adrift in a crowd of our friends, gazing across the bar at the copper distillery equipment in the background. A classmate touched me on my elbow, then hugged me and stood back. "You look good," she said, taking in my three weeks postpartum shape in my maxi dress, the one I'd picked because I'd calculated that its stretchy cross-wrap top would allow for somewhat discreet nursing, "for having just given birth."

A long-haired woman turned around and approached our

group, and I saw in a flash that it was Dina, another grad student in English, her three-month-old cuddled up against her in a fabric wrap. He peeked his head out, calm, peaceful, alert. That was what I'd thought my motherhood would look like: my life, my friends, and the baby in it with me, content and hanging out.

But now, after a few weeks at home with my own fussy infant and my achy swollen body, I looked at her baby and felt like I was in the presence of some marvelous foreign creature. I'd heard that babies could be like this—awake but not screaming—but I hadn't seen it from my own yet.

I tried to chat with her, make jokes about how I hoped in looking at her peaceful baby, I was looking at my own future. When she and her husband asked how we were doing, I tried to tell stories that were funny but also honest—the time the doula was supposed to come help with breastfeeding but canceled because someone else was in labor, and I was so desperate I cried all morning! Soggy tears all over the baby's head while he was nursing!—but none of my wild-eyed jokes quite managed to land. It seemed there was an unbridgeable gap between us. Before we had our babies, we weren't close. I'd recognized her pregnancy in the halls of the department before I was sharing my own and felt encouraged that someone else was going before me. We'd briefly overlapped at prenatal yoga, though she was close to giving birth when I was starting the new session. But if I'd also hoped there would turn out to be some kind of connection after giving birth, that didn't happen.

Thinking of this now, I can see that Dina was the mother I'd intended to be, or that she looked like it. I asked her if she was going to Cuddlebugs, the group for new moms and babies at Happy Bambino. *Sometimes*, she answered, with a shrug. She didn't seem to be jumping out of her skin at home alone with a baby who wanted only to nurse and howl. She probably had a whole group text going with cool moms who met to talk about how much they loved co-sleeping and cloth diapering.

I wanted mom friends like that. I wanted to show those moms that I was one of them. I decided I'd start going to Cuddlebugs once I got this all under control. Once I was ready to be seen.

Child Care and the Growth of Love

In the WHO report that would launch his career, Bowlby described not just the necessity of a mother's care but the satisfaction a woman must take in providing that care. He wrote, "Just as the baby needs to feel that he belongs to his mother, the mother needs to feel that she belongs to her child, and it is only when she has the satisfaction of this feeling that it is easy to devote herself to him." Once a mother has achieved this easy devotion, she'll be able to care for her baby in the way Bowlby expects, which he describes in the following sentence: "the provision of constant attention day and night, seven days a week and 365 days a year." Even as she sleeps, the mother is mostly a person for her baby. This is the kind of mothering Bowlby meant when he named the paperback edition of his report *Child Care and the Growth of Love*.

To develop his WHO report, Bowlby spent five months traveling across Europe to meet with experts and observe the care of children in four different countries, then spent an additional five weeks in the United States. His journals and letters from the time, though, show that Bowlby's conclusions were largely predetermined before his journey began: whatever ills those children suffered, the mothers were almost certainly to blame. He'd been commissioned to carry out a research trip, but it was really more like a scavenger hunt, as he spent those months searching for findings that would prove what he already believed.

Before his departure, he wrote that he worried about "the danger of racketing about seeing too many people—half of whom [would] be pretty stupid." And as he traveled across France, the Netherlands, Switzerland, and Sweden, he happily recorded the information in alignment with his ideas about mothers as the source of their children's mental and physical health. When his findings ran counter to his theory, he seems to have essentially just put down his pen. One scholar characterized Bowlby's trip as an opportunity for him to share his ideas internationally and an optimal chance "to gather evidence that confirmed this view." For a scientist with rigorous training from his country's elite institutions, Bowlby had a curious predilection for selecting only the evidence that best suited the argument he'd wanted to make anyway.

Bowlby believed that only the mother could properly care for her child. He even coined a term for the precise way a child depends on his mother: monotropy. Bowlby, whose father had been a surgeon to the royal household for King Edward VII and King George V, drew on the example of the monarchy to illustrate the principle: "much as each of the subjects of the realm come to direct his loyalty toward the queen," so, too, the baby depends on his mother. Like heliotropy, the way a plant bends toward the sun as it grows, a child bends toward his mother. There can be no substitute.

It's perhaps not surprising that someone who began his trip by writing that it was "very doubtful whether I shall pick up much of value which I do not know about already" reported findings that aligned to what he'd believed before he set out. Since the late 1930s, Bowlby had been arguing that maternal care or lack thereof was at the root of child delinquency. Charged with examining the mental health of homeless children, he once again blamed mothers.

Reading this research, I always wonder why the scientists of the day spent so much time and so many resources theorizing about those children's inner lives and who could be to blame. Couldn't the problem of homelessness have been solved, in part, by *giving families homes?* It turned out the Swedes had taken this approach, and they paired psychiatric research with programs meant to address social factors like poor housing, unemployment, and parental addiction. The Swedish approach to supporting struggling children and families assumed the problem might be not in a mother's heart but in an empty pantry. Bowlby, unsurprisingly, didn't care for this approach. He mentioned it only briefly in his report.

Mother-Care

When my mother first visited, the baby was two weeks old. I was still bleeding, and my nipples had barely healed from those traumatic first days of breastfeeding. On the first full day of her visit, my mother came downstairs to find me emptying the trash, scrubbing the dishes, and loading them in the dishwasher. "You shouldn't be doing this," she said. "You don't have to do this. You should rest. You should let me help."

"I feel more like myself when I do this," I responded. My Self, as I thought of her then, was a person who washed the dishes, who wouldn't let them pile up in the sink like some kind of slob. My Self couldn't lounge on the couch while the baby sleeps, or spend whole afternoons staring into the baby's eyes or gazing at him while he slept in my arms. When the baby slept I needed desperately to read, to do research for my dissertation, to start working on new poems. My Self wouldn't let me rest.

I'd been so nervous to have anyone visit, even my mom. When we were just a few days home from the hospital, I sat on the couch with the baby, surrounded by the pile of pillows I used to get him positioned for nursing, and cried. "I don't want anyone to see me like this," I told my husband. "And it's not like they can really help, anyway."

I'd wanted my mother to come see our perfect baby, to see me as the competent, self-assured mother I'd been sure I would be. But my mother knew me. She could see my exhaustion, how it was making me sharp and tense. The next day, when the baby went down for a nap midafternoon, my mom insisted that I lie down, too. Wrapped in the darkness of our bedroom, with the baby sleeping heavily in his Pack 'n Play beside me, a deep sleep quickly took me, and I woke hours later, my head full of fog. When I went downstairs, my mother was in the kitchen, the air full of steam from her cooking. A pot of beef vegetable soup simmered on one burner, and on another burner, meatballs bubbled in jarred spaghetti sauce. A meatloaf was baking in the oven. Over the years, my father had given me pieces of my grandmother's silver—a sugar bowl and creamer at my bridal shower, several sets of coffee spoons, a large pitcher, all emblazoned with her monogram—and I'd stored them in a china cabinet I'd bought with a coupon at the St. Vinny's on the west side. My mother had pulled the silver out of the cabinet and laid it out on the long island in the kitchen, and she was polishing it all.

"I didn't know what you needed," she said, "so I just did everything I could think of."

"Fathers Have Their Uses Even in Infancy"

Rereading Bowlby's work now, his insistence that a good mother would not only devote herself entirely to her child, but feel totally fulfilled by that work—it seems an idea that could only have been invented by someone with very little practical experience of the day-to-day care of a baby. That work is beautiful, yes, and full of joy and wonder, but it's also exhausting and sometimes lonely and often just boring. Bowlby, a man who spent his life in clinics and conferences, studying mothers and telling them what to do, seems to have almost no knowledge of the ongoing labor of mothering and what trying to do that work alone could do to a woman.

But: Bowlby did have someone in his life who was endeavoring to help him understand the realities of those early postpartum months. His wife, Ursula, recorded her own experience of early motherhood in wrenching detail in the letters she wrote him during the first year of their first child's life. Bowlby had married Ursula in 1938, and their daughter Mary, the first of four children, was born in February 1939. Mary's first year coincided with England's entry into the war, and while Bowlby continued working in London, Ursula moved outside London to stay with her mother and brother. Though Bowlby intended to visit each weekend, he was often unable to travel to see his wife and infant daughter more than once every other week.

In this way, Bowlby repeated the parenting practices of his own father, who had often been away in his childhood, and who, even when home, typically spent only an hour or so on Sundays with his children. A few years after his beloved nanny Minnie left the family, Bowlby's parents sent him and an older brother off to boarding school, an experience Bowlby found traumatic.

Into his seventies, he was still talking about the horrors of that early boarding school experience, and he was frequently quoted as saying he "wouldn't send a dog away to boarding school at age seven." For a man who didn't like to talk about his childhood (Ursula wrote in her journals that she'd understood early in their relationship that talking about his family was "tabu"), he shared that story widely. It's clear Bowlby believed the way he was raised, the way many children of his class and time were raised, was harmful. But instead of being a different kind of parent himself, he devoted his career to telling women how they might mother better.

Through that first year and into the rest of their marriage, Ursula wrote to Bowlby while he was away, and her letters during Mary's first year reflect all the anxieties and strains of early motherhood, particularly for a woman who was raising her child with only her husband's occasional presence. While still in the hospital after Mary's birth, Ursula wrote, "I am very unhappy. The feeding is going badly . . . I get so tired by the evening that my milk goes. Visitors make me tired, but I am so lonely and on edge with only seeing Nurse all day." Later in that first year, Ursula wrote to Bowlby about the claustrophobia of caring for a baby, exclaiming that "half the day I feel a great longing to get away from my baby and this room, and to be running or walking somewhere out-of-doors. Or to meet people again and talk about the war, or books or something other than the baby." Ursula's letters, though they were written eighty years before my own entry into motherhood, mirror so closely my own feelings in those months. When I was inside the house with the baby, it seemed I could feel the whole world speeding by outside. Ursula wrote to her husband of her loneliness, the demands of motherhood, how much she missed him when he couldn't visit and how hard she found it, when he did visit, when he returned to London.

This separation wouldn't have been unusual during the war, and though I'm inclined to find fault with Bowlby for those missed weekend visits, it's not fair to extend my present-day expectations for fathers into the past. What does strike me, though, is how vividly Ursula presented the hardships of that time, and that her voice seems not to have entered his consciousness at all. Ursula seems to have known this; in her journal, she wrote, "I'm sure he would accept useful concepts from trusted colleagues, without hesitation. He certainly wouldn't from me." Bowlby had written, in *Maternal Care and Mental Health*, that "fathers have their uses even in infancy," with the father's role being to support his wife emotionally so that she could give herself over entirely to caring for the baby. But, judging from Ursula's letters, Bowlby seems to have fallen short of even this meager expectation.

They wrote huge volumes of letters, but Bowlby and Ursula seem to always have been speaking past each other. And in those achy first weeks, I felt like I was always talking, a constant gush of feelings and tears and breastmilk, but it seemed that Smith simply couldn't hear me. One afternoon, after I'd gotten the baby to sleep in his bouncer, I went to stand in the doorway of Smith's office and tell him we weren't doing it right, he was supposed to be sleeping flat on his back, he was supposed to be falling asleep on his own. I'd read all the sleep books and blogs and the baby might be sleeping *now*, but surely the tricks we were using spelled trouble for the future. I just can't see it, I told him, I can't see how we're going to get there. (Where did I think we were going? I wonder now. To some longed-for future where I was doing it right, where I'd finally feel like a good mother? I know now that ending never really arrives.)

Smith looked up, finally, from his keyboard, maybe sighing a little. He'd heard all my complaints and worries for weeks now. "It's just a phase," he told me. We'd get through this part, then we'd be on to something else. The more wound up and anxious I got, the more he settled into a steadfast calm that only made me feel crazier. He wasn't wrong, of course. But his cool reassurance couldn't reach me. Just a few years after Ursula wrote those heartrending letters, in his landmark paper on attachment theory, Bowlby would write confidently that "it is fortunate for their survival that babies are so designed by Nature that they beguile and enslave mothers." Despite having been told by his wife, over and over, in writing and no doubt in person, he seems not to have ever thought about what it might feel like to be thus "enslaved" by an infant.

Baby Dates

As summer wound toward fall, friends prodded me out of the house with the baby. On Tuesdays, I met Ana and Lauren at 4 & 20, a bakery a few blocks from my house, for coffee and a pastry. Some days I arrived sweaty and desperate, with a screechy baby who'd cried inside the wrap or squawked from his stroller the whole way. Some mornings the baby slept in his stroller while we chatted, but more often, he fussed and whimpered and Ana and Lauren took turns holding him so I could eat more than one bite of a muffin at a time. Some days I'd have to text that I'd be late, or that I'd miss entirely because the nap was going long. On one of those mornings, they brought a breakfast sandwich right to the house and sat in my living room. I was too tired to have much of anything interesting to say, but it was so wonderful to not be alone.

Spending that time with Ana and Lauren helped me to see my baby. At home alone with him, he still seemed largely like a mysterious stranger. I couldn't tell what he wanted most days, except that I knew he didn't seem to be getting it. But Ana saw him growing and changing. "Eyebrows!" she exclaimed one day, noting the change in his expression.

One Thursday evening we were sitting at the picnic tables outside the Malt House, a bar in our neighborhood, where the baby was beginning once again to work himself up. I'd fed him, changed him, waved a toy toward him. Nothing seemed to help.

Lauren reached for him, and I happily handed him over. She cradled him and draped the swaddle across her shoulder so it lightly covered him. "He's overstimulated," she said, as she rocked and shushed him. I'd read about overstimulation in the baby sleep books, on the blogs. I knew it meant a baby who was trying so hard to take the whole world in that he was getting overtired but couldn't sleep. I couldn't recognize it in my own baby until someone else showed me.

He began to settle in her arms. I didn't know what my baby needed. But, for the first time, I felt relief. I didn't have to figure it out all on my own.

Our babies come to us so tiny and so helpless. It's hard not to want to be whatever they need. I can see the appeal of becoming a baby's sun. It's the most acceptable form of power most women can access. And what's the alternative? To refuse to bend and soften and meet your baby's needs, whatever they may be?

But it's a false choice. The alternative to attachment isn't abandonment. You don't have to choose between being an endlessly devoted, constantly available mother or leaving your baby in the back garden and sending your seven-year-old off to boarding school. The alternative is sharing the work.

Father Knows Best

Like Bowlby, Harlow devoted his career to studying mothers and babies and left the care of his own children to others. Harlow was also a father of four children, two sons with his first wife and a daughter and son with his second. He'd married his first wife, Clara, in 1932, two years after they'd both arrived at the psychology department at the University of Wisconsin, Harlow as an assistant professor and Clara as an ambitious graduate student. Clara was brilliant. At fourteen, she'd been selected for Lewis Terman's study at Stanford of gifted children, and she graduated from high school and entered Mills College in Oakland, California, at fifteen. At first, it seemed Harlow was drawn to that intelligence. In a letter to her family, she wrote, "When I began making A's in physiological psychology, Harry Harlow began escorting me home."

Marrying Harlow, however, meant the end of Clara's academic career. Wisconsin, like most universities at that time, had a strict policy against nepotism. This meant that a university would never be able to hire both of them, and even that early in his career, it was clear that Harlow would always be chosen over her. Clara's advisor told her to quit the program, reasoning that she'd never get an academic job. Even aside from Wisconsin's nepotism rule, women faced an uphill battle in the workforce. It was still legal at the time to refuse to hire a woman simply on the basis of her sex, and women were regularly fired for getting pregnant. Clara got a job at a downtown department store as a sales clerk.

They seem to have had happy years, but by the time their second son was born in 1942, Clara was at her wits' end with Harlow's absences from home. She begged him to spend time with their sons, insisting that if Harry was going to spend his weekends at the lab, he at least take their older son, Robert, with him. Robert remembered those trips fondly, following his father through the monkey house. Those grudging Saturday parenting sessions weren't enough to hold their marriage together, though, and in 1946 Clara filed for divorce. She moved the children to Rhode Island, where her brother lived. Robert would later say his younger brother had no memories of their father from childhood.

Harlow also met his second wife in the lab. Peggy was an ambitious assistant professor who had earned a PhD from the University of Iowa and spent two years at the University of Minnesota before coming to Wisconsin and joining Harlow's research team. They snuck across the border to Iowa to get married and didn't disclose their marriage to the university, in an attempt to skirt the nepotism rule. But eventually word got out, and when it was clear that one of them would have to go, there was no mystery about who it would be.

After Peggy was forced to resign, Harlow found her an office in the lab, where she became an unofficial—and unpaid— editor, tasked with polishing manuscripts for Harlow and his grad students. When Harlow was named editor of *The Journal of Comparative and Physiological Psychology*, he enlisted her help. She remained a serious researcher, and they were co-authors on a number of papers. Unlike Clara, who packed picnic lunches for employees in the lab, Peggy was no-nonsense at work. She could be cool and brusque, with one former student describing her later as an "ice bitch."

Though Bowlby was certain that a mother's employment would spell disaster for her children, Harlow allowed that a woman *might* be able to manage both work and motherhood, provided that once she was home, she was really home, fully engaged with her children in the evenings and on weekends.

In his second marriage, Harlow remained as obsessive about his work as he had been during his first. He worked long hours at the lab, drinking early morning coffee with the janitors and staying until nine or ten at night, though, as his longtime secretary Helen LeRoy pointed out, in her reminiscence of her years working with him, he did go home for dinner.

Presumably, it was Peggy who left the lab early to cook dinner, clean up after, and handle bedtime with their children. Jonathan, Harlow's son from his second marriage, would later describe his father's obsessive focus on his work and his comparative lack of attention to his children. "My father had had children before us with Clara," he said. "I don't think he was that interested in us." Of course, Harlow hadn't been that interested in the children he'd had with Clara, either, and after they moved to Rhode Island he saw them only when he happened to be traveling near them for work.

Some of the scholars writing about Harlow excuse his virtually nonexistent parenting, saying he was a product of his times, as if fathers hadn't been invented yet. And it's certainly true that our expectations for hands-on parenting from men have changed since 1942. Harlow did, however, have people in his life at the time trying to tell him they needed more from him: his wife, his children.

The point is not that Bowlby and Harlow were inattentive parents. History is full of bad dads. Rather, it seems that despite all those hours in the lab and the obsessive devotion to the research that led him to argue about the centrality of mothers, he failed to listen to the mothers who were speaking to him. A woman's voice, telling the truth about her life, is a form of evidence, too. The science is worse for that inattention.

. . .

Clara had left graduate school after her second year, the same stage of my PhD program at which I became a mother. Before the baby was born, I'd thought less about how I'd manage the workload of teaching and a dissertation alongside caring for a baby and more about how I'd be perceived once I was visibly pregnant. That fall of my pregnancy, I sat in graduate seminars quietly nauseous, and by spring, when I had a Friday morning class at College Library and a belly expanding by the week, I walked past tables of undergrads bleary-eyed from all-nighters feeling like a cautionary tale about unprotected sex.

There are rules in the writing world, in academia, about how many kids to have and when to have them. If you had to have a baby, you'd better wait until after tenure and stop at one. Wanting a baby—wanting something with your body—was in opposition to the life of the mind. One friend, a professor at a nearby university, told me a story about her own experience with pregnancy in academia. She had been in graduate school when she got pregnant with her first child, and when her advisor saw her in the hallway, he took one look at her visibly pregnant form and said, "Oh, that's too bad, you were so serious about your work."

It takes only one story like that to cast a long shadow down the whisper network of ambitious young women. And though pregnancy discrimination of the kind that was entirely legal in Clara and Peggy's day has long since been outlawed, a recent *New York Times* investigation found that it "remains widespread." The gender wage gap is, in many ways, really a motherhood wage gap, as each child costs their mother, on average, a 4 percent reduction in hourly wages. In contrast, men's wages increase, on average, 6 percent after becoming fathers. This parenthood pay gap persists across Europe and Scandinavia, where a recent study shows that, despite family-friendly policies including parental leave, high-quality government-subsidized daycare, and flexible workdays, mothers working full time still make on average fifteen to twenty percent less than men. So much for solving all our problems by moving to Sweden.

· · ·

I don't know what Clara wanted. Maybe she really was happier, for a time, at the department store, than at home with her sons. When pregnant, she wrote to her mother that "I do not agree with women who take six weeks off to have a baby." She was determined to get to know her child first before handing his care over to anyone else, though she suspected, she told her mother, that another job would find her in time. So perhaps, had she not been forced from her PhD program by Wisconsin's nepotism rule, she might have still chosen to leave. But I know the choice was taken from her.

I wonder what Clara might have discovered, had she been allowed to continue in her studies. I wonder what we've lost by edging generations of brilliant women like her out of the lab and back into the home.

The years since Clara's short-lived graduate studies have given us some answers to this. When "the second wave of feminism had opened once-closed laboratory doors" and women began to enter the sciences in bigger numbers, zoologist Lucy Cooke argues, they upended a century's worth of sexist assumptions and the bad science that had been built on them.

Since Darwin, men had known what to expect when they looked at female animals. "The males of almost all animals have stronger passions than the females," Darwin wrote in *The Descent of Man*. The female, on the other hand, is, almost without exception, more passive and "she requires to be courted." (You'll notice these female animals sound suspiciously like the ideal mother of Darwin's day, the self-sacrificing woman who lives only for her husband and children, who has no intellectual or sexual desires of her own.) Across the animal kingdom, the thinking went, female animals were the same: submissive, monogamous, devoted mothers. Nothing to see there, really, and so scientists from Darwin on mostly didn't look. Mothering in particular was understudied—seen as "'the home economics' of animal behavior," anthropologist Sarah Blaffer Hrdy explained in her book *Mother Nature*.

When scientists did study mothers, they mostly did it in the lab. In Bowlby and Harlow's era, comparative psychologists studying maternal behavior filled cages with mother rats, hamsters, cats, and other animals, each mother isolated with her offspring. The scientists removed all the variables and all the stressors, the need to find food, the possible distractions and disruptions from other animals, to study motherhood in its essence. This experimental setup bears a striking similarity to the ideal suburban housewife, home alone with her small children. Each mother rat performed for the scientists a highly specific version of what it means to be a "natural" mother. In these experiments they're relieved of the pressures to find food but also stripped of social context. The scientists kept check sheets recording instances of the behaviors they'd defined as maternal: suckling, licking, carrying the babies, hovering over them as they grew. The scientists could not observe (and would not have cared to note, in any case) behaviors that didn't fit with this vision of the devoted maternal animal. These caged mothers had no chance to forage for food or compete for status. They had no other mothers with whom to share the caregiving. The scientists had made a caged paradise for them: mother, baby, freed even of the need to secure their basic needs. As if a good mother could want only her own babies anyhow.

Bowlby and Harlow looked at the animals that suited them, and they saw what they'd expected to find. In a piece published after his death, Harlow described how he came to select rhesus monkeys as his research subject. He'd begun his primate research with orangutans and a baboon, animals that had persuaded him of the power of nonhuman primates as research subjects. Unlike rats, they had easily discernable personalities and preferences. They formed relationships with researchers, and they showed that animals could learn complex lessons and problem solve. It seemed so obvious that we could learn lessons from those primates and extrapolate them to humans.

But the large apes were an impractical choice for laboratory research. When it came time to develop his own research program, with his own animals, Harlow had to select a smaller animal that would be amenable to life in the lab. While he'd previously worked with a selection of different species, disciplinary pressures, which Harlow described as "a constant trend among psychologists toward more formal and rigid experimental designs," meant he needed to select just one species for all his studies. For a time, his lab contained an assortment of small monkeys, which Harlow loved for their whimsical, individual personalities. The cebus monkeys, spider monkeys, and chimpanzees had big personalities, but Harlow ultimately landed on the rhesus macaque for a practical reason: it contained, as he put it, "a central nervous system waiting to grind out a hundred test trials a day." Those rhesus newborns became our models for human babies not because they were the closest model for humans, but because they were the most convenient test subjects. In fact, Harlow notes, anthropoid apes like chimpanzees are certainly more intelligent, "but they seldom become such ideally, automatic, unquestioning, problem solving machines as the monkeys." The rhesus monkeys were also better suited to the climate of the Upper Midwest. Neither cebus nor spider monkeys, both New World monkeys from South America, could survive the conditions of the lab, which was designed with access to outdoor cages; in contrast, rhesus monkeys grow a thick fur coat that could carry them through the harsh Wisconsin winter. Visitors to the lab, Harlow wrote, "often marveled at the sight of monkeys playing in the snow." In other words, the rhesus monkeys were chosen for their suitability to laboratory life and their willingness to endure the highly repetitive nature of experimental science, rather than their ability to tell us anything about ourselves. Harlow and the many people who've written about his work since then made the leap from monkey infant to human mother anyway.

Baboon Mothers and Others

One scientist, Jeanne Altmann, decided to look more closely at mother baboons. In 1971, Altmann and her collaborators began a longitudinal study of baboons in Kenya's Amboseli National Park that continues today. Female baboons have the curious and potentially deadly habit of kidnapping the infants of lower-status females. Because baboons must nurse frequently, even a brief interruption can be lethal, and because female baboons have a rigid social hierarchy, lower-status females are most at risk. But Altmann discovered that these low-status female baboons had developed a strategy for protecting their babies: friendship. This friendship, developed through the social currency of grooming, releases endorphins and reduces stress. And these networks of baboon friends work together to protect their offspring from danger and identify food sources to share. In the end, Altmann found, these friendships can be even more powerful in safeguarding infants to adulthood than higher rank. Counter to Bowlby's ideal all-powerful mother or Harlow's self-sufficient cloth mother, the baboons cared for their children by mothering together.

Altmann's baboon research was revolutionary for not just what she looked at but also *how* she looked. She insisted on recording everything, and not solely, as so many male scientists had before her, what she expected to see.

Reading about those baboons, I think about the single moms, my mother and her sister, who raised me. For a time, after my parents divorced and my mother, sister, and I moved to Pittsburgh, my mother was working long hours in her office downtown, working to prove herself competent and worthy of the position she'd pursued all through graduate school. It was the late eighties, and she was a single mother, riding the bus downtown in stockings and sneakers, her pumps kept beneath the desk in her office. We didn't know anyone else without a father in their house; we knew almost no one else with mothers who worked. The mothers who worked mostly did so part-time, or they were teachers and able to be home when their own children finished school. We'd moved to Pittsburgh from State College, where my parents had met at Penn State, to be closer to my mother's sister. We moved to the same suburb and for a time my mother and aunt shared childcare for the four girls they had between them, each pair of girls two years apart so that we made a stepladder of ages.

On Thursdays my mom worked late, and we went to my aunt's house and ate Tuna Helper and watched *The Cosby Show* and sometimes slept sideways, all four of us lined up across my aunt's king-sized bed. They lived in an old house in an old neighborhood with cobblestone streets, and there was a little TV room on the second floor where we could watch TV without anyone peeking in on us, so my sister and I flipped the channels to things we weren't supposed to watch, like Nickelodeon and MTV, shows our mother worried would make us talk back. The house had a curving set of stairs and an old wooden banister and an attic. We had Easter brunch in that house, eggs Benedict with béarnaise, and Christmas dinner with roast beef my grandmother brought from the butcher in her small town in northern Pennsylvania. At daycare we were *the cousins*, and at that house I was as at home as in my own.

The shared labor of working motherhood. How long could that have lasted? For a time we had shared babysitters after school and in the summers, and a few were awful, but mostly they were indifferent to us, and we ran through the house and into the backyard, a world of our own making. Like so much of childhood, it feels like it went on forever, but it must have been only a few years. My aunt remarried and moved to a different house on the other side of the city. A few years later, my mother remarried and we moved to a different house as well, the townhouse my new stepfather had bought when he divorced just a year or so before. He'd furnished it with solid-colored comforters and framed illustrations of ducks, surely not expecting to have a new wife and two more daughters moving in so soon. By coincidence, the new house was near my aunt's new house and we went there sometimes. They bought a computer and a printer before we did, and I went there on Sundays in middle school to type my papers in the cool basement that opened out into the backyard. I had my awkward first kiss, with a boy whose only real merit was that we shared a bus stop and a love of Pearl Jam, in the backyard at my cousin's birthday party one spring. But it was never the same, not really, the flowing between houses, the easy sense of being at home.

The women remarried and once there were men, we mostly stayed in our own homes. The division of labor solidified inside each house. We'd been baboons. Then we were rats again.

Writing a Happy Infancy

After a summer inside with the baby, the calendar ticked toward fall and the start of a new semester. In late August, the baby almost two months and still not sleeping, I went to campus for the department welcome-back event. I'd won an award for a scholarly essay I wrote, a revision of the doctoral exams I'd written through my pregnancy. I stood in the conference room where I'd attended this same event the previous three years in a row, where I'd sat for countless meetings and workshops, but in the haze of sleep deprivation, I felt I hadn't really arrived. My body was still somewhere outside the room. Or, I'd brought my body and my brain hadn't come along yet. The conference room had windows overlooking Lake Mendota, and I watched the sailboats making their way to the shore. The room felt too bright, all the people I knew from years of classes and parties and beers on the terrace replaced by familiar-looking strangers.

When the time came to receive the award, my classmates

coaxed me to the front of the room. I stood before my advisor for a moment, blinking, before he told me to shake his hand. I did my best impression of a woman who'd written several thousand continuous words that apparently merited recognition. I was trying to travel back to that part of myself that believed I was a writer.

Though Ursula is most often depicted as the ideal wife and mother, the living embodiment of attachment theory—one biographer referred to her as the "secure base" from which her husband was able to set out into the world and do the real work of scientific discovery—she must have felt the flare of ambition, too. Ursula had been a serious writer since childhood, and she began a degree at the University of Edinburgh, but when her parents' marriage ended, she returned home to spend time with her mother. As a child, she'd written poems and stories, and after marrying Bowlby, she wrote articles on breastfeeding, discipline, and pregnancy for parenting magazines.

When Ursula's papers were handed over to the Bowlby archive at London's Wellcome Library, they consisted of fifteen boxes spanning the years from 1926 to 2000. The first fourteen boxes included letters and diaries, but the fifteenth contained a surprise: the manuscript of *Happy Infancy*, a book Ursula wrote on early childhood. At the time she wrote it, many British mothers were influenced by Dr. Truby King, a New Zealand parenting expert who advocated for putting babies on strict feeding schedules and leaving them largely to their own devices, alone in a crib in the nursery or in the back garden, between those feeds. Ursula's book, in contrast, encouraged mothers to reject these rigid schedules and follow their own instincts in caring for their children. Ursula wrote the book in the late 1940s and revised it in the early fifties. Over the same years she gave birth to four children while her husband traveled across Europe and the US and shared his research at conferences and in newspapers and magazines and on the radio and made a name for himself as an expert on mothering, Ursula, too, was writing a book. She would not see it published in her lifetime.

· · ·

That August afternoon, as I was standing by the elevator to the parking garage, my advisor from my MFA stopped me to ask how I was doing, if I was writing about the baby. I can't remember what I said, or if I answered him at all. But inside I thought: How could I write about the baby? I was *caring* for the baby. Nursing, pumping, wiping, washing and drying onesies, keeping myself a little fed: that took every ounce of brainpower I had. Where was the poem in that? What could there be to say about the baby, and what version of me could say it?

3

An Ordinary Devoted Mother

I sat in the blue gray of the nursery in the middle of the night, pinned beneath the nearly sleeping baby, as shadows moved across the plaster swirls that swooped along the walls. The cream rug was nubbly against my bare feet. Beads of condensation dripped down the side of the glass beside me. Each night when I put the baby down, I'd place a glass full of ice on a coaster on the side table so that when I got up with him later, I'd have cool water to drink while I nursed. That night, when the baby had woken, I'd fed him, changed his diaper, then laid him down on the floor to swaddle him again, pulling the fabric across his arms and chest, then yanking the final fold tight to turn him into a snug little bundle. Now, he was tired but fighting it. He rubbed his nose against my neck, whimpering and muttering like he had just one more thing to say before he fell asleep.

From my spot in the corner beneath the baby, I could see Smith walk from our bedroom to the bathroom. I heard a stream of piss hit the toilet bowl, a flush. His body appeared again in the doorframe, and he walked back to bed without looking at me, as if I, too, were a piece of furniture or the sleeping lump of a baby. I didn't need anything, or I didn't need anything he could give me, but I wanted to be asked. In the nighttime, he cared for his own needs, then went back to sleep. I was tethered to the baby and his needs, the boundaries of my body blurred by nursing. My husband was lying back down to sleep, and I was a cord of flame, my rage flaring in the dark nursery.

We'd never talked about how we'd share the work of caring for a child. At our childbirth classes, we were given a worksheet one night listing different chores related to childcare, everything from feeding and diapering to making doctor's appointments and researching daycares. The couples were given time to talk about how they'd split the work. We shrugged it off. We didn't need to be so formal about it, we'd figure it out when we got there. Except for a rough stretch when we'd first moved in together and Smith was unemployed and I'd lost my mind after coming home from work to a sink full of dishes, we'd never talked explicitly about the division of household labor. We got along so well. We were happy. And if everything inside the house gradually ticked over to my side of the chart, and if the work inside the house just grew and grew, I could handle it. That was what it meant to me, then, to be a feminist and a mother: to be the competent and independent one, the one doing all the work. This was the version of second-wave feminism I'd inherited from my mother. I didn't need a man. I'd absorbed that I could have it all as long as I was willing to do it all myself.

And also: the baby had been my idea. I wasn't sure I was allowed to ask for help.

· · ·

Penn snorted and nestled against my shoulder, not yet solidly asleep. I'd read online that a baby needed at least ten minutes to fall into a deep sleep, so I counted down the green digits on the alarm on the top of the bookshelf above my head. I knew that if I put him back down now, he'd wake, and we'd have to start the count all over again.

At my baby shower, months earlier, my mom's best friend Mary had told me that she loved being up with her babies at night, that she cherished caring for them in a way that only she could. Alone with the baby in the night, I wanted to feel like Mary did, placid and drowsy and full of love. But when I got up to nurse, I didn't feel like I was special to the baby. I could have been a faucet or any warm mammal. I did not feel loving, and I did not feel loved.

• • •

Before those long nights in the nursery, we'd had a few good weeks where it seemed like things were getting better. I'd read all the sleep books my older stepsisters had recommended and started a nighttime routine: feed, bath, book. I was working on gentle sleep training, not the full-on cry-it-out kind that natural parenting folks said could damage your baby and his bond to you. The big goal was to get the baby to go down sleepy but awake, so that he'd learn to fall asleep on his own. By mid-October, as the baby passed three months and started sleeping in the crib in his own room, he was going down without much fuss and sleeping a reliable long stretch from 6:00 P.M. to 2:00 or 3:00 A.M. When he'd been in the Pack 'n Play beside me, I'd startled awake every time he rustled or grunted. Now that he was across the hall, I slept deeply for the first time in an eternity, certainly since his birth and the achy late-pregnancy weeks that preceded it. My dreams were thick and vivid, as if my subconscious were working to make up for all that lost time.

Those hours of connected sleep returned my brain to me. I met with my advisor at a coffee shop, started drafting a dissertation proposal, went to meetings at the campus writing center. We hired a babysitter, and she came for three hours at a time Monday, Wednesday, and Friday. I planned a birthday party for myself and spent a whole Saturday's naptimes baking, cooling, and frosting a three-layer chocolate cake. We sat with friends in the living room while the baby slept upstairs. We drank champagne. They sang, and I blew my candles out.

We've got this figured out, I thought. *This is going to be okay.*

Near midnight, after we'd said good night to friends and stacked the plates in the dishwasher, and I was just about to lie down to sleep, the baby woke up screaming. It was too soon. That first period of sleep, all the websites and experts said, was always the best, and every interval after that would be shorter, fractured.

That night marked the beginning of a sleep regression that went on for months, the baby waking as early as ninety minutes or an hour after he'd been put to bed, so that there was no time to sleep before he woke and needed me. It didn't seem like he could possibly be hungry again, but nursing was the only thing that would soothe him. For months, it seemed, as soon as I clicked off the lamp on my nightstand and put my head down on my pillow, he'd start crying across the hall. We joked that he could tell, that he was doing it on purpose, but some nights, when all I wanted was to sleep, when I wanted one night where no one needed me, it didn't feel like a joke.

Happy Children on the Radio

Seventy years before and across an ocean, the voice of an anonymous doctor drifted into women's kitchens each Friday morning as part of the BBC's *Happy Children* series. For his first talk, "Getting to Know Your Baby," in December 1943, he began by assuring women that, whatever their hopes and hobbies had been, even if they'd been uninterested in babies or dismayed by the restricted lives of their friends who'd become mothers, motherhood was their destiny. Every woman, he insisted, even those with "wide interests," even those who'd been engrossed by business or politics or tennis, would eventually arc toward motherhood. "Sooner or later," he announced, "she herself becomes pregnant." And with this inevitable pregnancy, he explained, those formerly wide interests would narrow in scope, until "she slowly but surely comes to believe that the centre of the world is in her own body." By the baby's birth, the mother has turned her gaze from the outside world to the child whose care is about to consume her. The doctor described how a new mother could get to know her baby in their earliest days by insisting, against the practices of the day, that the nurse bring her baby to her even between feedings, so she could become accustomed to his moods and his different cries. This devoted attention would set mother and baby up for a contented relationship and start the child on a path to becoming a confident, independent adult. But it was vital that the mother do this work herself. "The care of a newborn is a whole-time job," the doctor intoned, and it is one that "can be done well by only one person."

That anonymous doctor would soon be revealed to be Donald Woods Winnicott, whose radio addresses in wartime Britain and the decades after provided guidance to generations of new mothers. During the war, the BBC had fashioned itself as "the voice of Britain," and its programs were played in homes and bomb shelters. It's hard to imagine a single media outlet having this kind of reach now, but at the time, nearly 50 percent of the UK tuned in for the BBC's 9:00 A.M. news bulletin. Across more than sixty talks on the BBC, many of which were turned into pamphlets and eventually books, Winnicott would have reached a wide swathe of British homes. His most famous series, *The Ordinary Devoted Mother and Her Baby*, became a popular book by that same name whose fans included Ursula Bowlby. In 1957, during the same period when she was working on her own book, Ursula wrote to Winnicott to express her admiration for *The Ordinary Devoted Mother*, noting that "it has been the only English book which I've felt able to recommend when mothers have asked me for the name of a good baby-book." Winnicott had been trained as both a pediatrician and a psychoanalyst, and his Freudian-influenced theories about childhood and early infancy reshaped young mothers' ideas about what a baby needed and how a good mother would meet those needs. Though Winnicott had been largely unknown to the general public at the beginning of the war, by the end of the war, as a result of his radio broadcasts, he was "a renowned public figure."

When Winnicott began his radio talks in 1943, he was addressing women whose lives had been wracked by war. Many would have had husbands stationed overseas, and many would have been themselves doing war work and trying to keep their own children fed through rationing and safe despite bombings. Nearly eight million British women, almost half of them married, were in paid employment by 1943, a dramatic increase from the 16 percent of married women in the workforce a decade before. And even for those less directly impacted by military service or a spouse's absence, the war was everywhere, something Winnicott would have experienced as well. As Winnicott traveled to the BBC's studios in central London to record his contributions to the *Happy Children* series, he'd often have to drive through "the glass and rubble of the previous night's air-raid."

Born in 1896, Winnicott was himself engaged in war work for the second world war of his lifetime. After graduating from Cambridge, he'd joined the Royal Navy in 1917 and become the medical officer on the HMS *Lucifer*. He'd write later, in his private journals, about the devastating impact of the losses during that first war. "So many of my friends and contemporaries died in the first World War," he wrote, "and I have never been free from the feeling that my being alive is a facet of some one thing of which their deaths can be seen as other facets: some huge crystal, a body with integrity and shape intrinsical in it."

As World War II began, Winnicott was especially concerned about the impact on children. When the British government began evacuating children from urban areas to the countryside in an attempt to keep them safe from bombings that targeted cities, Winnicott joined with John Bowlby and another psychiatrist in a 1939 open letter protesting this policy because they believed that separating children from their mothers was a psychic harm that would follow them for the rest of their lives. Despite this protest, Winnicott was recruited to work in the hostels that housed the most troubled evacuated children. The majority of the children evacuated from urban areas were from the lower classes, and they would be housed with middle-class families who'd been forced to take them in. In many cases, the evacuated children were treated as servants, and if their behavior proved too difficult for the reluctant host families to handle, they were sent to hostels. Winnicott was charged with supervising the care of three hundred evacuated children across five such hostels in Oxfordshire. Winnicott seems to have relished this wartime work, writing shortly after its end that "I hardly noticed the blitz, being all the time engaged in analysis of patients who are notoriously and maddeningly oblivious of bombs, earthquakes and floods."

While he was working in Oxfordshire, Winnicott met the woman who would become his second wife, Clare Britton. Clare had trained at the London School of Economics, where she'd told her classmates that, rather than working in a clinic, "I want to be in the hurly burly of what's going on in the world." When Clare arrived in Oxfordshire, Winnicott was first described to her by the hostel staff as "a difficult doctor." "He comes down and talks to the children," they told her. "He plays his pipe to them and we like him very much, but he doesn't ever tell us what to do."

Clare handled Winnicott in a way that would set the precedent for the rest of their work together. Since Winnicott was uninterested in providing guidance to his staff, she suggested they simply charge on as best as they knew how, and when he next visited, they could ask if he had any suggestions. Her approach had the genius of not depending on Winnicott to do supervisory work he plainly didn't want to do while also appearing solicitous of his stature as the supervisor. In this way, Clare established an innovative practice of professional collaboration with hostel staff, including the foster parents, social workers, and psychiatrists, all working together on a fairly equal footing. Clare and Winnicott wrote the first of many co-authored articles, "The Problem of Homeless Children," based on their time together during the war.

. . .

Winnicott's work with those evacuated children must have influenced his wartime addresses to mothers. In addition to talks on issues that are universal to life with an infant, like the first weeks with a new baby, understanding your baby's cries, and feeding and diapering, he also addressed problems that were particular to the traumas of the time, like his two-part series on "The Evacuated Child" and "Return of the Evacuated Child."

During the war and after, the BBC claimed an important role for itself as a force for normalization in British families. The same concern that had motivated the WHO to send John Bowlby on a research trip around Europe and the United States to learn about children's mental health led the BBC to devote a significant portion of its programming to children and mothers. Much of this programming, including Winnicott's talks, was guided by psychoanalysis and its understanding of childhood as a vulnerable state that would influence the entire rest of a person's life. As one historian put it, "Psychoanalysis was not only high theory; it also had very real implications for public debate and social policy." Winnicott was particularly skilled at distilling (or dumbing down, depending on your perspective) complex psychoanalytic ideas for a broad radio audience. His audience had been raised on a different tradition entirely, one marked by rigid scheduling and less strain over a baby's every whim and need, one that did not freight mothers with the sole responsibility for their child's psychological health. The fact that he was able to convey the key ideas of psychoanalysis, which placed the mother at the center of her child's emotional life, without using Freudian jargon no doubt contributed to his success.

Though many of Winnicott's ideas—his vision of the infant as already a unique person, his insistence that mothers learn their own babies' personalities and preferences, rather than following a rigid feeding schedule—were progressive for their time, his overall vision of family and gender roles was deeply regressive. Mothers grew ever more important, even as women themselves were increasingly seen only as vehicles for the health of their children and thereby the nation. And, as the institution of motherhood took on central importance, women themselves receded into the background of public life.

Because he entered British popular culture first through the radio, his voice filling the rooms where women cooked breakfast and fed children and washed dishes, Winnicott developed an especially intimate relationship with his audience. Winnicott's voice was high and thin, so much so that some women hearing him on the radio mistook him for a woman. Some scholars have theorized that his voice took on that timbre from years of speaking to mothers and babies, as if women who've given birth must themselves be spoken to with baby talk, as if only a softer sound can reach them in the country of babies. His biographer blamed the women who'd surrounded him in childhood—two older sisters, a mother, a nanny, a cook, aunts across the road—while his father appeared only once a week, when they walked the ten minutes home from church together.

Whatever the cause, that quality seemed to have worked to his advantage as his voice floated into those morning kitchens, keeping women a discreet kind of company. I imagine them tuning in to the radio as they wiped the kitchen table, as they counted down the minutes to lunch and naptime. And they didn't just listen—they talked back, writing in to the BBC in droves, sometimes hundreds of letters in response to a single talk. When they wrote to him, they addressed him not quite as an expert whose advice would direct them, but as a sympathetic ear, someone with whom they might share their experiences and hardships. They shared their stories—nurses who wouldn't let them hold their own babies in the maternity ward, a mother-in-law who hovered but didn't help. One woman, a grandmother, wrote in to say that nursing her babies had been the sweetest part of her married life. Winnicott, in contrast with many of the other parenting experts of his day, told mothers that they already knew what to do. "No book's rules can take the place of this feeling a mother has for her infant's needs, which enables her to make at times an almost exact adaptation to those needs," he reassured his listeners.

There's a puzzle in this, of course. If mothers already have built-in intuition to guide them, why do they need a man on the radio telling them what to do?

The Child, the Family, and the Outside World

Though Winnicott has assured his listeners that once they knew they were pregnant, once their baby had been born, their thoughts would all turn to their baby, mine didn't. I loved the baby, but I itched to get back to work. I was desperate to write. When a friend sent out a mass email with an invitation to join in writing a poem a day for two weeks, I immediately signed up. I scrawled notes during afternoon naps and typed up the poems after bedtime, then sent them out into the email chain, feeling the slick click of accomplishment as I checked each draft off my list of tasks. I pumped milk and ducked out for meetings on campus. Even as the baby grew and smiled and seemed finally to know me, my ambition didn't still. I didn't want, as Winnicott reassured his listeners they would, to stay inside, lulled by love for my baby. He'd expanded one set of talks into a bestselling book, *The Child, the Family, and the Outside World*, the title of which always seems to me to suggest that the mother and her baby belong inside, that they're a domestic unit distinct from public life. But I wanted so much to get back into the world.

I wasn't teaching that fall semester, but I was working as a research assistant for a professor in my program and tutoring at the writing center. I tried to complete my research tasks during naps or sitting in Smith's office while he worked and the baby grumbled in the Rock 'n Play between us. A couple days a week, I drove with the baby to the YMCA, where I could get two hours of free childcare at Child Watch. I'd buckle the baby into one of the swings lined up in a row along the wall, then zip upstairs and run on the treadmill, one ear cocked for announcements. Child Watch wasn't really daycare, and they didn't do diaper changes or give bottles, so if your baby needed something, they were quick to call you back. On days when I made it through my run without being called, I'd grab a bench in the women's locker room and click away at research work for my professor. That makeshift workstation in the locker room always felt illicit, like I was stealing time from someone. I didn't know how else to get it all done.

On Sunday nights, I nursed the baby, then drove to campus for my writing center shift. I tutored in a dining hall on campus, where I ate ice cream made of milk from university cows and talked to students about their key words and their thesis statements and their signal phrases. Once, carried away with the freedom of three whole hours away from home, I swapped the soft shell of my nursing bra for a pre-pregnancy bra and in that evening interval, the underwire did its work. Hours later, I woke in the middle of the night, sweating and chilled, symptoms, the internet told me, of a plugged duct. Awake alone in the night, I took a hot shower so the steam could loosen the dense knot of milk around my nipple, then sat in the gray light of our guest bedroom and pumped to unblock it, crying from the pain and the stupidity of my mistake, thinking I could go out for three hours dressed as a woman without a child.

I kept our babysitter's three-hour shifts clear for writing. As soon as she walked in the door, I rushed out, driving to a coffee shop where I wouldn't be able to hear the baby, where my breasts wouldn't thump and leak when he cried. I couldn't think when I was in the house with him, but at the coffee shop I got my brain back. When I could, I claimed a window seat, perched on a high stool at the counter facing the street. I was a dissertator now. I'd finished my coursework and passed my exams before the baby's birth. But I'd heard too many cautionary tales of grad students before me who'd spent years fine-tuning the proposal before sputtering out, and women especially who had babies and stopped writing, who seemed to just float away from the seminar rooms where the dissertators shared their work once a month at writing group. I developed the theory that a dissertation was like the great white shark, which, if it stopped moving, would suffocate and die. I was terrified that if I put my work down now, I'd never be able to pick it back up.

But also: I loved my work. I was writing about the Wisconsin Rural Writers Association, a midcentury group devoted to encouraging rural people to take up creative writing to record their stories and folklore. The group's scrapbooks, magazines, and newsletters were held in the university archives, where I'd spent hours poring through brittle yellow pages and making scans of anything promising. Those files were full of ordinary people, farmwives and schoolteachers, describing what writing and being seen as writers meant to them. I used an emerging set of theories, new materialisms, to think about everything that had to come together to make a writing practice possible in a busy life: not only pen and paper, but the postal service that circulated drafts for the round-robin correspondence writing clubs, the newly improved rural roads that brought members together, sometimes across large distances, and the blizzards that often forced them to cancel. My brain buzzed with those new ideas. And, though I wasn't aware of it at the time, the material circumstances of my life—the haze of sleep deprivation, the tiny notebooks I kept everywhere in case a thought popped up while I was trapped beneath a sleeping baby or walking to the park, the rhythm of frantic typing while Penn was with the babysitter followed by enforced breaks when I returned home—all of that was shaping my writing practice, too.

On those mornings at the coffee shop, I felt like I was inside a display box: woman writing. I typed fast, one eye on the clock. The words whipped together with a speed I haven't matched since. As I wrote, I faced forward so that even when I saw friends or classmates they would know not to interrupt those precious paid-for hours.

Never Good Enough

Today, Winnicott is best known for coining the phrase "good-enough mother." That idea has been translated to us through pop psychologists and Instagram posts to mean something like "You've got this, Mama." It's been taken to mean that you don't have to be perfect—you can just be "good enough." As long as you're trying your best, this translation goes, you're doing great. This idea of "good enough" has come to seem like a way of relaxing, of lowering our expectations. But that's not what he meant.

Winnicott's good-enough mother makes a series of minute

adjustments as her baby grows. She fails her baby, but strategically, incrementally, so that he can begin to learn he is a being distinct from his omnipresent mother. Nowhere in the theory is there any consideration of what the mother might need or feel. And it isn't necessarily the case that all mothers can be "good enough." In the paper articulating this theory, Winnicott wrote that "mothers who have it in them to provide good enough care can be enabled to do better by being cared for themselves." However, "mothers who do not have it in them to provide good enough care cannot be made good enough by mere instruction."

My heart always sinks when I read that second sentence. Some mothers just don't have it in them to be good enough. Some mothers can't be helped.

I tried so hard, in those months of night wakings and skull-splitting exhaustion, to get help.

Before the birth I went to classes on childbirth and babies, breastfeeding and baby wearing. I went to prenatal yoga and watched our bellies grow in the mirrored room alongside Lake Mendota. After giving birth I went to two different lactation specialists. I read up on infant massage and considered cutting out dairy when I read that some sensitivities could be passed through breastmilk. I went to a workshop on pumping. I went to my first postpartum checkup at four weeks, the date the nurse had insisted I schedule, though my doctor sent me away after a brief conversation, saying it was too soon for an exam, and I returned three or so weeks later, where the doctor declared my single stitch had healed up nicely. I went for a baby-carrier fitting, I went to have my pump checked when I wasn't producing enough milk to fill even the smallest bottles.

I never went to anyone to talk about how I was feeling. I never even thought about it.

The help I sought out was all professional grade, aimed at transforming me from an ordinary woman into a mother. I was trying to learn the rules and best practices. I believed that if I could learn the right way to bundle the baby into his wrap I'd look like the good mother I intended to be, that if I could get my breasts to produce for the pump I could keep up breastfeeding once the baby started daycare like all the guidelines said I should. I believed that I was the one who needed fixing. In none of those workshops and appointments did it ever occur to me that maybe the problem wasn't me.

And in almost none of those spaces did anyone ever really see me.

No one ever said, *Maybe you should talk to someone.* No one ever said, *Let me make a call for you. You seem like you feel bad and you don't have to.*

. . .

There was one striking contrast: ten weeks after the baby's birth, I signed up for a postpartum Pilates class that met on Monday evenings. We sat in the back room of the natural parenting store, the same room where I'd spent so many summer mornings at the breastfeeding clinic. For Pilates, the furniture was all pushed to the edges of the room. At the first sessions, I sat on the floor with a group of women in yoga pants, and I realized when we started chatting that I was by far the newest mother in the room. One woman with a two-year-old talked about how they were still co-sleeping and she hated it but couldn't figure out how to stop. Another woman with two children in preschool talked about how hard it was to make time for herself, how she wanted to exercise more and finally lose the baby weight, but she couldn't fit it in between work and kids.

If these women, years in, were still so beaten down, what hope was there for me?

The instructor asked us each to share our birth story. When it was my turn, I started my story by sobbing, which surprised me, because the birth was the one thing I felt I'd done well. I'd followed my birth plan—low-intervention, no drugs for pain relief. That roaring birth, those peaceful three days in the hospital were the last time I'd felt like a good mother.

Another woman in the class gently told me about the postpartum depression group, how the group helped her work through those first dark months of motherhood. I'd seen photos of that group on the store's website. I'd looked at those women and thought, *It's good that they got help*. I didn't think that their faces had anything to do with me. My bad feelings—the way my whole body buzzed when I was away from the baby, the tightening across my chest when he cried—didn't belong anywhere in what I understood to be the domain of postpartum depression. Postpartum depression had been explained to me as an extension of the "baby blues," and I'd imagined it as a kind of photogenic weeping, selflessness made of love for the baby. So when my bad time didn't feel like that, I figured that what I had was more like Postpartum Being a Bad Mother or Postpartum Being an Asshole Who Shouldn't Have Had Kids Anyway. It would take me years to learn that postpartum depression is just one condition on the spectrum of postpartum mood and anxiety disorders with complex and varied symptoms. Even today, postpartum mood and anxiety disorders frequently remain undiagnosed and undertreated, amounting to what Postpartum Support International calls "a silent health crisis." Because I understood my own feelings as a personal failing, I didn't know how to ask for help.

It was only later that I could hear what that mother at Pilates was saying: that I was one of them, too. She was being gentle, but she was saying: *I can see that you are struggling. You should get help, and this is how.* In all those months, the only one who really saw me was a fellow mother. And I couldn't hear her.

The Plunge

That exhaustion in those months of sleep regression made my brain strange to me. It cracked me open. Once, deep in the night, as I crossed the hallway into the nursery, my brain crackled and I felt the theoretical framework for my dissertation snap together.

In the daytime, I scanned my copies from the archives, I checked my ideas against the theories. I assembled my arguments and my evidence. This was how I'd been trained, all those years in grad classes, to say, *What is the story, what is the evidence?* You can't just make any argument you want.

I'd been trained to have big ideas but look for proof. And this is what I love about qualitative research: you get the rich, granular details of a life, then the quantitative data that provides the context. That kind of work asks: What is your story, and what sense do you make of it?

Listening to Winnicott's arguments about how mothers feel, what they want, I keep thinking, *But how do you know? Where's the proof?* It's the question of the seminar rooms where I spent years discussing articles and learning jargon and raising critiques. With Bowlby, the answers are clear. He shows his work, even if his methods for gathering that evidence are selective and unrigorous. With Winnicott, in contrast, even as I read and re-read, his logic seems to shimmer before me. He's so confident, so declarative about what babies need and how easily mothers can give it to them. But where's his evidence?

This question isn't academic. Winnicott's work has shaped what we think early motherhood should feel like. When the women I knew talked in glowing tones of the sweet love of early motherhood, how suddenly staring at their sleeping baby was more fulfilling than work or friends or any of the things that occupied them before giving birth, they were channeling Winnicott's voice. When we lionize mothers as having superhuman strength that allows them to feed and dress the children, pack cute lunches and remember spirit days, and track their children's shifting moods and needs through maternal intuition, and when we attribute all that to mothers' natural goodness rather than a lifetime of being socialized to care, we're living with the consequences of those ideas. In Winnicott's first radio talk, which described motherhood as the ultimate destination for every woman, he explained that some women, on first learning of their pregnancy, might resent it as a "terrible interference with her 'own' life." The scare quotes are right there in the transcript, as if anything you'd been before your baby's birth was just a dress rehearsal, and anything you might be after becoming a mother would forever be simply a footnote to the real work of caring for a child. I imagine his voice lilting on the radio, addressing all those silly women who'd thought they had a self before they had a baby.

Winnicott believed that, for the ordinary devoted mother, the early weeks of motherhood would be marked by a state of such complete devotion to the new baby that it would be an illness at any other time in a woman's life. He had a name for it, primary maternal preoccupation, though on the radio he said this was simply "being occupied by your baby." According to

Winnicott, the new mother will "plunge" into primary maternal preoccupation, an "extraordinary condition which is almost like an illness, though it is very much a sign of health."

The ordinary devoted mother will find this absorption in her baby effortless, he explained, but not every mother can do it. There are two ways to fail at primary maternal preoccupation: by not being devoted enough, and by becoming too focused on the baby. In Winnicott's words, "at one extreme is the mother whose self-interests are too compulsive to be abandoned," meaning she cannot immerse herself fully in the baby. But the mother who becomes too focused on the baby is a danger, too, if the baby becomes her "*pathological* preoccupation." There are so many ways to do it wrong and such a slender needle to thread if you're aiming to do it right.

For Winnicott, the newborn mother lives in a watery world of love. When pregnant, the blood inside a woman's body doubles in volume to make the quart of amniotic fluid in which her baby floats, and after giving birth, she'll produce up to thirty-five ounces of breastmilk a day. The way Winnicott describes a new mother's love sounds so much like drowning. If an ordinary mother feels like her baby has pulled her under, how are you supposed to know if you need help?

• • •

Earlier that summer, when the baby was still tiny, my sister had called, sounding nervous, and told me there was something she needed to talk to me about. I was standing on the landing of the second floor, just outside the nursery where the baby was napping. "Give me a minute," I said. "Let me go downstairs."

I paced the kitchen, the tile cool against my feet, as my sister explained: someone she'd known in high school, who'd married the younger brother of someone I'd gone to school with, a whole tangle of families and people I'd never known well but who'd all stayed in Pittsburgh and stayed close, she'd had a baby. And she'd been having a really hard time, my sister explained. She'd asked her doctor for help, but she'd been told that if she was admitted to a psych unit, they might take her baby away, even though she had a husband, even though she had a whole web of extended family who could help. If she continued, if she needed this kind of help, she'd likely lose her baby.

"She killed herself," my sister said. "And I know you've been having a hard time," she said, her voice breaking, "so I just want to make sure you're okay."

I reassured my sister: It was hard for me, but not like that. I was okay.

But I thought about that other mother often through that fall. Her baby wasn't quite six weeks old when she died. Each time my own baby reached a new milestone, as he became more and more a person to me, as he began to know me, I thought of her. When he smiled, when he began to smack his doughy little hands in excitement, when he drifted off to sleep after nursing without drama, I thought, *It gets so much better. And she'll never get to see this.*

. . .

What would Winnicott have said to her? Would he have patted her arm and told her to listen to her instincts, that she knew best what her baby needed? Would he have been able to hear her?

I think about all the women his voice reached on the radio. At first, I picture them in quaint midcentury kitchens: wearing an apron, maybe sweeping the linoleum floor after popping dinner in the oven. There's a baby in the high chair, maybe an older child playing with a train set in the living room.

But some of those women must have been like that mother in Pittsburgh, or like me, seriously struggling and feeling like no one could hear them. What would Winnicott's voice have sounded like to them?

Some mothers can't be helped.

• • •

What was Smith doing, in the bed beside me, while I huffed and sighed each time the baby's cry rang through the monitor beside my head? Was he alert and listening for the baby, too? Was he tuned to the crackling frequency of my anxiety? Was he just going dark, knuckling down, getting through it?

I'm sure he believed that he was helping. On Saturdays he took the baby so I could go to the gym and write at a coffee shop. I went to book club and he stayed home with the baby. Every time I asked for help, he did it. He never complained. But I still felt like the baby was my job, and in those long nights in the nursery, I felt like I was doing it alone.

What would better help have even looked like? It's so hard to say.

I probably would have benefitted from medication to turn down the buzz of anxiety, talk therapy to work through my feelings. It would have helped to have someone to sit beside me in the dark, a schedule to share the night feedings so I wasn't always the one who had to get up.

But even more than that, what I needed were better ideas. I needed to believe that I deserved help, that I wasn't a failure for not floating through those early months of motherhood unscathed.

The First Mrs. Winnicott

It's an irony, or at least a surprising fact, that Winnicott, who devoted his life to the care of children, had none of his own. He had an unhappy first marriage, which, according to his biographer, was never consummated. (One source for this very personal bit of information was the analyst Winnicott saw for ten years of treatment, who wrote to his own wife about the Winnicotts' sexless marriage, which was just as much a breach of ethics in their time as our own.) By the time he married Clare, in 1951, she was forty-five. There's some evidence that they wanted children. There are records that they underwent fertility testing, though the odds, given Clare's age, would have been against them. I wonder if Clare felt the ten years between the probable beginning of their affair, in wartime Oxfordshire, and their marriage—years during which she might have had children, with Winnicott or others—had slipped away. Despite the long affair, Winnicott left his first wife, Alice, only after two heart attacks and the death of his father, who considered divorce a sin and whose disapproval likely dissuaded Winnicott from pursuing divorce earlier. Winnicott told Alice he was leaving her after twenty-five years of marriage over lunch, then went back to his office to see a client.

Alice is, in most accounts, the difficult first wife, tucked away in suburban Surrey while Winnicott was out in London doing the real work, the wife who had to be shucked off before Winnicott could fulfill his true potential. She's frequently characterized by his biographers as a troubled artist, prone to hallucinations and delusions. After I've read this description enough times, I finally recognize the trope: she's the Bertha to

Winnicott's Mr. Rochester, the crazy wife hidden in the attic, until Clare, his Jane Eyre, can save him. Winnicott's biographers note the dramatic increase in his productivity after his second marriage, as if Clare's adoration turned the faucet of his genius. Across the twenty-five years he was married to Alice, he wrote only one book, a textbook on pediatrics, but after marrying Clare, he published six more books and wrote enough lectures, papers, and correspondence to fill twelve more volumes that would be published after his death. In those stories, Alice shackled him, and once he freed himself, he flourished.

In one article, a serious Winnicott scholar, himself a psychoanalyst, speculates that Winnicott's first marriage remained unconsummated because Alice, whose father was a gynecological surgeon, may have stumbled upon her father's medical texts as a young girl and developed as a result a "fearful" understanding of female anatomy, "something disease-ridden, waiting to be cut with a knife." "Perhaps," he continues, "Alice even experienced her husband Donald—also a doctor—as having a knife-like penis which could inflict some horrific damage upon her."

"One can readily imagine," he writes, how a girl like Alice might come to be afraid of sex, which feels to me like it sums up all of midcentury psychoanalysis, with its obsession with women's shortcomings and its refusal to actually ask them what they think. I can *imagine* all kinds of things, and that's not the same thing as proof. I could offer a dozen more likely suggestions for why a couple isn't having sex that wouldn't require wild unsubstantiated speculations of a woman gone for more than fifty years, a woman whose voice is so thinly in the record it's all but impossible to hear.

Those stories shortchange both women, making Alice a

burden and Clare merely a muse. Clare, a skilled social worker and teacher in her own right, was actually the first one to recognize many of the concepts that would become Winnicott's landmark contributions to psychoanalysis. While he was theorizing, Clare was working directly with children and families. She'd learned, during the war, that if children had with them some familiar object from home, like a blanket or a toy, it lessened their distress. Winnicott would call this a "transitional object" and get the credit, but it was Clare who spotted it first. Hilariously, Winnicott was so certain that he alone had discovered the idea of a security blanket that he once wrote to Arthur Miller to ask if his children's book, *Jane's Blanket*, had been inspired by his theory of the transitional object. In that letter, he also mused that perhaps Charles Schulz, creator of the *Peanuts* comic strip, had given Linus his blanket for the same reason. Miller responded that the book was inspired not by Winnicott but by "observing my own daughter as a child."

Clare is often described as the muse who helped Winnicott achieve his true potential. But it seems more accurate to see Clare as not muse but partner, not a meek helpmate but a collaborator. Many of the ideas were hers, so perhaps some of the words were, too.

Clare was the competent one, devoted to her husband in his lifetime and to his legacy afterward. But it's Alice I keep wondering about.

Alice married Winnicott in 1923, when she was thirty-one and he was four years younger. By then, Winnicott had completed his medical training and become interested in psychoanalysis. Alice had attended Cambridge, following her mother and her older sister, during the decades when women were allowed

to study but would not be granted degrees or allowed to partic-
ipate in the full life of the university. Newnham College, where
she enrolled, was founded in 1871 as a women's college. Twice
in the years before Alice's arrival, the issue of whether women
could be granted degrees was put up to a vote, and twice it was
voted down. The second vote, in 1897, culminated in a riot as
crowds of men filled the street of King's Parade and marched
toward Newnham College. On their way, they ripped the doors
and shutters off local businesses to gather fuel for a huge bonfire
lit in Market Square. When they got to Newnham, they hung
an effigy of a female undergraduate on a bicycle from an upstairs
window. (I imagine at least some of those men, before stomping
off in a rage, would have said women were too emotional and
irrational to ever be their intellectual equal.) In 1921, after Alice left, there was another vote, another riot. No woman would
be granted a Cambridge degree until 1948, when the Queen
Mother was recognized with an honorary Doctorate of Law.

Alice spent her years at Cambridge doing the same coursework as men and taking the same exams, the same demanding
Natural History course, and she left without a degree. There
were other universities in the UK at the time that granted
women degrees, but the women who attended Cambridge were
ambitious, drawn to the prestige of attending such a selective
and storied university, even if it meant being awarded, at the end
of their studies, not a BA but a Cambridge "certificate." In those
years, women's exam scores were not ranked alongside the men's,
but the two lists were posted publicly, and the women's colleges
took great pride in how often their students' accomplishments
matched or exceeded the men's. After she left Cambridge, Alice
worked for five years at the National Physical Laboratory, where

she carried out research into ceramics and optical glass. In the only picture I can find of her, she's young and pretty, her dark hair pinned up. She's looking directly at the camera.

• • •

What had Alice hoped for when they married? One biographer notes that, given the shortage of men after World War I, securing a husband was "quite a considerable achievement." But Alice, before her marriage, had already accomplished so much: an education, a job, the beginning of her career as an artist. From the beginning of their marriage, Winnicott was almost constantly away, traveling into London six days a week to work with sick children and their families. Alice continued working in those years, exhibiting her art at the Royal Academy and the Royal Cambridge Academy. For nearly a decade, she owned a pottery studio in Kent, where she designed a line of dinnerware that was sold in a department store in London. During the war, while Winnicott was working alongside Clare in Oxfordshire, Alice was working in the war effort, too, offering art therapy at the Mill Hill School Hospital. It's hard to square all that accomplishment with the image of her as the wild-eyed, hysterical wife holding Winnicott back.

In that same period, Winnicott developed a habit of sending the most troubled children from his practice to his home and expecting Alice to care for them. He recounted in an article the case of a nine-year-old boy sent from London during the war "not because of bombs but because of truancy." After running away from the hostel repeatedly, the boy lived with the Winnicott family for what he described as "three months of hell." "It really was a whole-time job for the two of us together," Winnicott explained, which was of course complicated by the fact that

Winnicott was so often elsewhere, leaving Alice to do this two-person, full-time job by herself. Winnicott notes that "when I was out the worst episodes took place." It's hard to understand why, if Alice was as fragile and ill as she's always described, Winnicott was sending troubled children home to her care.

. . .

Alice had her own life, her art, and a suburban home; she wouldn't be, like Clare, the woman to hang on her husband's every word when he spoke about his work. Perhaps she wasn't the wife Winnicott thought he was getting. But how many of us are?

Marriage has for so long been a really bad deal for women, particularly those who want things beyond home and children. Alice doesn't seem the kind to iron her husband's shirts, though Winnicott did thank her for copyediting his first book. From this vantage point, Winnicott seems like just one more man who married a brilliant woman, then worked for years to make her less than she had been.

One biographer suggests that it was his extensive psychoanalysis that allowed Winnicott to make a better choice in his second wife, as though both women were bottles of salad dressing that he plucked from a shelf. Never once, in an article full of speculation about Winnicott and Alice's sexual dysfunction and Winnicott's eventual "potency," sexual and otherwise, does that biographer consider what either woman might have wanted.

Clare, presumably, got what she wanted: a career, a successful husband who loved her madly. No children, though if she'd married in her twenties, as was the average for her generation, she might have been one of the women listening to Winnicott in her kitchen, instead of traveling and lecturing alongside him.

And Alice? What might she have wanted? There are so few

records in her voice, it's hard to say, but maybe: a husband who would take her work seriously, who wouldn't leave her all the time, who at the very least might fuck her and stop sending home the children too troubled even for institutions with the expectation that she'd care for them when he was gone.

...

I keep searching for Alice. In one of her paintings, a tree's reflection stripes through a pond. In another, her sky is wild and full of movement, thick streaks of paint leaping across the horizon. She was an ambitious woman in a time when women's ambition didn't count for much.

My own ambitions thrummed beneath my skin. The baby split me open with love and wonder. At first, the baby was a mouth, all howl and hunger. But then he was all eyes, the world lit up with his attention. A dog, turned leaves blazing in the gray sky, the pattern of the crib slats against the nursery wall—he'd swallow the world with his looking. One afternoon, I sat beside him on the living room rug while he tried again and again to roll from back to belly. He swung his legs and rolled, but each time he'd get stuck on his right shoulder. He groaned and grumbled. He'd almost make it, the duck appliqué printed on the butt of his yellow jammies visible as he rolled, then gone again. I lay beside him on the floor and tried the move myself: Which muscles would it take to roll? He had such intensity and focus as he practiced each new skill. It was riveting to watch.

But I wanted so much beyond my baby. I drafted my dissertation proposal, sent it to my advisor, revised it, scheduled a defense. I remember almost nothing about the day, which should have been a milestone. I sat before my committee in my advisor's long, narrow office with his wall of windows facing trees. They must have asked me questions, and I must have answered them, written down their feedback in the notebook I'm sure sat open before me. I remember that my writing felt like a polished box. All those snug citations, the precisely articulated research questions and chapter outlines, all my terms defined. I mostly felt the smug satisfaction of speed: I'd had a baby, and I'd finished my proposal faster than anyone else in my year. Those words feel now like they were written by a stranger.

· · ·

Is it unfair to criticize Winnicott for leaving an unhappy marriage, Bowlby for being so often away from home, Harlow for devoting himself to his work and ignoring his children? They were, we imagine, men of their time. They're not much older than my own grandfather, who told my mother almost proudly that he'd never changed a diaper. It's so hard to reach into the past and make sense of what we find there, rather than what we wish we might see.

But also: they helped to make that time. The ideas that haunt us now—that women are designed by biology and evolution to nurture, that a good mother wants to care for her baby all on her own, that she naturally knows precisely what to do—can be traced back to these men. Bowlby and Harlow shored up our long-ambient ideals with science, and Winnicott set them out into the air.

The postwar years could have been, in the UK and the US, a revolutionary time. Women had gone to work and sent their children to state-supported childcare. Harlow argued that his research on love and contact comfort showed that fathers could be good monkey mothers, too. But that finding was overshadowed by the more dramatic image of the adoring cloth mother, who looked so much like Bowlby's sun-giving monotropic mother and Winnicott's ordinary devoted mother. Each of those imaginary figures was lit up by love for her child, her ceaseless, uncomplaining caregiving made possible by the magic of maternal instincts.

And where is the mother in all this research? Those men were eager to make grand proclamations about what a baby needed and what the consequences would be if a mother fell short. But what might a mother want, or need? The mother was simply whatever the baby required. In all this research, the mothers were, as one scholar put it, "the great absentees."

· 4 ·

Strange Situation

On a Monday in early January, we drove to the baby's new daycare. The morning was so cold that ice had formed on the inside of the windows in our old house, and I'd warmed the car in the driveway for a full ten minutes before taking the baby out. He was buckled into his car seat, a heavy car blanket crocheted by a friend who'd made it as a Christmas present tucked across his belly. One of the rules I'd memorized while pregnant: no jackets or snowsuits in the car seat because you couldn't pull the harness tight enough to make sure it would be safe in the event of a crash.

The baby's new daycare was an in-home center run by a woman named Cathy, who lived in a little ranch on Madison's north side, near the airport and just past the stadium where we watched farm league baseball in the summers. Cathy was in her sixties, divorced with two grown daughters. She was slender, with dyed hair that was dark and always a bit frizzled around her face. I'd packed for the baby's first day, outfitting him with extra jammies and two sleep sacks and a white noise machine to help him nap. An insulated lunch bag filled with bottles of pumped breastmilk, small Tupperware containers of home-made baby food. A gallon storage bag filled with little bags of frozen breastmilk, just in case.

When we arrived, Cathy was baffled by my preparations. She looked at the huge tote bag of supplies, perplexed, then at the cooler bag and the bag of frozen breastmilk. "Oh, I don't think I have room for all that," she said. A bit abashed, I unpacked the bottles and the Tupperware from the cooler bag and placed them in the fridge, took back the frozen milk to store again in our basement freezer.

For so long, I'd been beside the baby through nearly every mood and need. In the fall, the babysitter had cared for him in small chunks of time, but I was always aware of those intervals as stolen hours, always watching the clock, watching my word count as I worked, my breasts growing full against my shirt as I entered the second hour away from my baby. But I was headed back to teaching now, on campus three full days a week, and the baby would be away from us in those hours.

I'd found Cathy by luck, thanks to a referral from another grad student in the department. In early October, we'd gone to visit on a Saturday morning. Even on a weekend, the house smelled like soup and baby wipes, the heavy but not-unpleasant smell of years of children. As we sat at her kitchen table, she reached her arms out for the baby, who sat with her happily while she talked about the babies' routines, the nap schedule and the toys she'd rotate every week or so, the worksheets she used with the older kids so that they all knew their letters and num-bers before they started kindergarten. Cathy ran the daycare by herself, and she'd cared for countless babies over the years. Through the kitchen window we could see the play area in the back, a fenced concrete pad with a slide and a playhouse, where the kids could play in good weather.

Cathy felt a bit like someone my grandmother would have known, though she must have been closer in age to my mother. One Monday, when I told her we'd taken Penn to the Madison Children's Museum downtown over the weekend, she told me that the last time she'd gone downtown, she'd gotten stuck in a parking garage and had to call security to get her out, so now she didn't go *all the way down there* anymore. (Madison is a tiny city. She could have, from her house near the airport, been on the Capitol Square in twenty minutes and paid eighty-five cents an hour to park in a covered garage.) Once she was cooking her own dinner in the late afternoon as parents were arriving to pick up their kids, and I told her it smelled good. "It's a recipe my mother-in-law taught me," she said. "Want to know the secret? I cook the chicken *with garlic*," she confided, as if naming an exotic spice.

On that first day, I handed the baby over to Cathy. PBS was playing on the TV in the playroom. Mateas, the other baby, was sitting in a Jumperoo and fussing a little. Cathy reached over to pat him, reassuring him that she'd get to him next. He wasn't happy, but it wasn't an emergency. It was nothing like when I was at home with the baby and every whimper felt urgent, like a problem that was mine to solve. But here, all those kids wanted something, and they'd all be fine.

We walked back down the narrow hallway and into our red Volkswagen, already chilled after sitting in the driveway for just a few minutes. We left the baby inside.

• • •

At home, without the baby, the house felt impossibly still. I had a syllabus to finish, a dissertation to write, but in that quiet,

I wandered through the kitchen and the living room. My husband worked upstairs in his office, clacking at the keyboard. With every creak in the old house, I was alert, sure I'd hear the baby crying, needing me. But he was elsewhere, across town, where another woman held him, gave him a bottle, spooned yogurt and applesauce into his mouth before he napped.

I felt the baby's absence, but I didn't feel bad. Daycare felt like freedom. The baby was happy, safe, cared for, and I could work, long stretches at a time, long enough to ride the bus to my favorite coffee shop, stare out a window, drop a thought and pick it back up again. Each day at pickup, Cathy gave us a little scrap of paper with the record of his day: how much milk he'd had, what he'd eaten, how he'd slept. The record of his little life away from us.

But should I have been so sanguine? Other mothers I knew ached when their babies were away from them. I remembered a woman I'd worked with years before, when I was teaching high school English, an intimidating woman who directed the curriculum for the entire district, rushing out of a meeting one day, saying she had to pick her kids up from the "strangers" who were raising them. I looked up, alarmed—strangers? They're at daycare, she explained. It had never occurred to me to worry about daycare like that. In my own life, as the daughter of a working mother, daycare had just been another place. We went, we came home. We were fine.

I'd soon realize that I was maybe not alone in that, but certainly not in the majority. What were the potential harms of daycare? It was nebulous, vague. There were some genuinely scary stories—babies left unattended, diapers unchanged. But I trusted Cathy. She was experienced, calm. The lurking danger was a psychological one, something that, acquaintances and strangers on the internet suggested, might lie hidden beneath the surface for years. A baby would surely be hurt by all those hours away from his mother, even if he was cared for in her absence, even if he was so small it seemed he couldn't really miss her.

In other words, wasn't I running a terrible risk, sending my sweet baby to daycare? Wasn't I flirting with turning him into someone who'd forever be insecurely attached?

Attachment: More Style than Substance

The concept of attachment styles has become so pervasive today that it feels less like psychological theory and more like an objective truth about the human condition. You can take a quiz to identify your attachment style, or to diagnose the attachment style of an ex whose inattention left you feeling unloved. You can find entire Instagram accounts devoted to explaining how your attachment style will influence your romantic life, your parenting, your friendships.

Underlying all this talk about attachment styles is the claim that what happens between a child and their primary caregiver in the earliest years will determine the quality of their relationships for the rest of their life. People whose caregivers fostered a secure attachment, the theory goes, have self-confidence, the ability to be both trusting and vulnerable, and the general mix of healthy self-esteem and careful boundaries that Instagram therapists insist is the secret to lasting intimate relationships. People whose caregivers were less reliable, or perhaps alternately attentive and rejecting, will face a lifelong struggle with anxious or avoidant attachment styles. Anxiously attached adults are driven by fear of rejection and abandonment and have tendencies toward co-dependency, while the avoidantly attached among us have difficulty sharing feelings and trusting others. Your co-worker who's clingy at happy hour? Probably anxiously attached, due to her emotionally distant or unpredictable mother. The boyfriend who takes forever to return your texts? He's not ghosting you, he has an avoidant attachment style. (In the least surprising twist of all, his mother is also to blame.)

There are so many good reasons to question the science underlying the neat conclusions attached to attachment styles, but in the realm of pop psychology, here's one, to start: these labels fall so consistently along stereotyped gender lines, with women often identifying as anxiously attached and labeling the objects of their unrequited affection as avoidant. If the science just reaffirms sitcom clichés, how much faith do we want to put into that science?

Attachment styles were first articulated by Mary Ainsworth, a Canadian American psychologist who had a decades-long collaboration with John Bowlby. Before attachment styles were pop psychology, in other words, they were grounded in actual psychology. (Attachment-obsessed as Bowlby was, he, too, was the subject of armchair diagnosis by a loved one he'd disappointed. Bowlby's older son, Richard, described his famously formal and somewhat distant father as having "an avoidant attachment style.")

Ainsworth developed the laboratory experiment that is used to assess a child's attachment style. In that experiment, the Strange Situation protocol, a child between nine months and three years old comes to the lab with their primary caregiver, and they're admitted to a room set up as a living room with various toys. After a few moments, a stranger enters, and a few minutes after that, the caregiver leaves briefly, then returns. The child's response to their caregiver's departure and return determines their attachment style. A child who's securely attached is distressed when their caregiver leaves but is easily comforted by their return. Securely attached children will also use their caregiver as a "secure base" to explore a new environment, perhaps running around a playground but checking in visually or by touch with their caregiver periodically to make sure everything is okay. In contrast, children labeled anxious-avoidant will refuse their caregiver's comfort, and children labeled ambivalent will show mixed signals on their caregiver's return.

And if you're reading this and thinking: *No fair! I'm not a baby, but I would love to have all my issues cataloged and tracked back to my childhood!*, don't worry—the attachment styles industry has got you covered. There's an Adult Attachment Interview, developed by Mary Main, a protégé of Ainsworth's, which in about an hour will cast its crystal ball backward to find the childhood roots of your present-day malaise.

This is the magic of the Strange Situation: twenty minutes in a lab, and any reasonably well-trained graduate student can identify a baby's attachment style, and from there, make determinations about the quality of the care he's been given in his life. There are genuine advantages to the kind of systematized approach to research the Strange Situation uses. Lab protocols like these produce a huge volume of data quickly. You can train graduate students to administer them. You can publish at speed. You can build a whole career that way.

None of that means the research tells us anything about life outside a lab. As one article, tellingly titled "Are There Really Patterns of Attachment?" put it, attachment theorists have paid little attention to whether the categories defined as attachment styles are "a true taxonomy," something with significance outside the protocol, or just "a mere measurement convention." You might feel like you're anxiously attached, in the same way you *feel* like you're a Libra or an ENTP, and that might help you understand how you move through the world—but that doesn't make it science.

One particularly odd feature of the Strange Situation is that the parenting is never directly observed, and researchers don't interview the parents or children they're assessing. Instead, the quality of their relationship is inferred from how the child responds to the protocol. Infancy researchers, one attachment theory proponent claims, regard the Strange Situation as "a Rosetta stone of sorts" that can be used to "decipher the traces of an infant's experience with his parents." But unlike the real Rosetta stone, the people who might help us decode the mysteries at work are right there. The protocol doesn't allow for a parent to describe their child or share any information about their life at home. Nowhere in the protocol is there space for researchers to inquire if the family has stable housing and enough to eat, if the child has faced developmental or behavioral challenges, or even if they've had a tough morning before arriving in the lab. Instead, the protocol treats child-caregiver relationships as a code that only the researcher can crack.

Because it's done in a lab, because the people who talk about it often have long strings of letters behind their names, the Strange Situation and attachment styles have taken on the glowy haze of science, with its promise of certainty and rigor. And that has consequences for the lives of ordinary families. Pop psychology aside, the Strange Situation, and attachment theory more broadly, has had a long reach into the lives of ordinary families through both culture and policy. Attachment theory has had a particularly strong influence in social work, and its assumptions about mothers have shaped social workers' interactions with struggling families, resulting in what one scholar of social work has called "attachment-driven interventions," which can "result in 'outcomes' that can be life-changing for children and families." For Black and Brown families and for poor families, who are more likely to have their parenting called into question by state agencies, not performing attachment correctly can have incredibly high stakes.

Attachment theory researchers assert that the message of their work is "simple and life-affirming." After all, they say, "the only thing your child needs to thrive emotionally is your emotional availability and responsiveness." *The only thing*, I think. The only thing your baby needs is you, your complete availability and responsiveness. And what if you have needs of your own, a desire to work or rest or pursue hobbies or friendships unrelated to the baby? And even if you really desire only your baby, what makes that possible? This research so often seems to assume that women and babies alike live outside their context, and certainly outside any kind of economic concerns. After all, aren't those essential, simple traits—emotional availability and responsiveness, continual devotion through every mood and stage and moment of the day—made possible through material things, like sufficient sleep, a safe and stable home, food, and electricity? Even if the baby only needs the mother, what about what the mother needs?

. . .

And make no mistake: the Strange Situation, like attachment theory more generally, is about mothers. It's rooted in the assumption that the mother is a being who exists only for her baby. Bowlby's influence on Ainsworth is clear in the design of the Strange Situation itself: a mother-infant pair, with the mother serving as a "secure base" and source of comfort when the baby is stressed by the stranger or the mother's absence. The idea that there will necessarily be a single primary caregiver is built right into the research design. And though the protocol doesn't necessarily define that the caregiver will be the mother, you can guess who's been tested. Defenders of Bowlby are quick to point out that he acknowledged, in a single footnote, the possibility of a "substitute mother-figure." But an honest reading of his work across his lifetime makes it clear that he believed that an infant needed one primary caregiver, that dispersing this care across multiple family members or caregivers in a daycare would result in lasting harm, and that the biological mother was the one best suited to that work. After all, if Bowlby had been thinking of a gender-neutral caregiver, swapping "parent" for "mother" would have cost him nothing in terms of either letters or syllables. He said *mother* in print and interviews throughout his life because that's what he meant.

But if you design your study starting with the assumption that the mother is the only thing that matters to the baby, does it really count as a research finding if that's what your study claims to prove?

Risky Business

Strange Situation research has often been used to make arguments about childcare in the first years of a child's life, with the supposed lifelong benefits of secure attachment held up in contrast to apparently less important things like a mother having a job or a life outside her home.

"Attachment-theory proponents tend to see full-time daycare in the first year as a risk," intoned Robert Karen in a 1990

Atlantic article that became the basis for his award-winning book *Becoming Attached*. And what's the risk? A mother whose baby spends more than twenty hours a week in "substitute care," Karen warns, is "running a serious risk of his becoming anxiously attached." This number comes from a study done by two Penn State researchers, which asserts that infants "exposed" to more than twenty hours a week of nonmaternal care are more likely to be classified as insecurely attached. It's not clear why twenty hours is the magic number used by that study, and I can't help but wonder if it's an amount that might allow a woman to keep her little part-time job, enough to earn some pocket money, but not so much that she might actually be competing with men for full-time employment. It particularly irks me to think that those researchers were doing that analysis during the years we, too, lived in State College, years my sister and I were in daycare while my mother was working unbelievably hard to advance in her career and care for her children, years she spent single-parenting and earning an MBA at night after spending all day at her full-time job. That those Penn State professors would have considered her anything other than an excellent mother boggles the mind.

And it's true that 1990 was a long time ago, but these ideas about the harms of daycare are with us still. Even now, little wars flare up across social media about daycare and mom guilt with surprising regularity, with one side claiming that daycare is necessarily damaging, that even if the center is clean and staffed by warm caregivers, even if your kid seems happy and loved, there's danger hidden just beneath. The defenders of daycare often do it in the most practical terms: that some people need to work, that research shows that high-quality daycare is fine.

But what often feels lost in all this is the idea that daycare isn't a necessary evil but an incredible benefit to children and families, a place where kids are taught and loved by people beyond their family, where they learn to interact with other kids and practice new skills. When we see daycare as a makeshift solution to the problem of a mother who insists on working, we end up with the patchy, inadequate marketplace of too-expensive options that plague us today. If we could imagine daycare differently, we could craft policy that would make high-quality childcare, subsidized by the government in the same way K-12 education is, available to everyone.

Despite how pervasive the concept is in psychology and pop culture, the research in attachment styles is all positioned on a remarkably precarious foundation. Once you start looking at the research, it feels less and less likely that a bunch of men (and the occasional woman, to be fair) in postwar England discovered the only right way to raise a child, and that it just happened to entail leaving all the work to a woman.

Unnatural Selection

Ainsworth first met Bowlby in 1954, when she worked with him at the Tavistock Clinic in London. She'd moved to London from Toronto, where she'd been an assistant professor in the psychology department at the University of Toronto. The Strange Situation, and Ainsworth's decades of rigorous laboratory studies, functioned as the empirical research arm for Bowlby's theoretical apparatus.

Bowlby had first defined attachment in his 1958 paper, "The Nature of the Child's Tie to His Mother," in which he mused at length on the wonders of a mother's love and the way mother and baby had been designed to be a perfect, self-sufficient pair. But the challenge Bowlby would face across his career was selecting evidence to support his claims. He maintained a clinical practice throughout his life, but seeing troubled children isn't the same as conducting systematic research, which he'd stopped doing after his 1944 "Forty-four Juvenile Thieves." As a result, he had to hunt around for others' research. (How you feel about Bowlby's choice to not conduct his own studies depends largely on how you feel about his work as a whole. Robert Karen, a psychologist and journalist, and a proponent of attachment theory, calls Bowlby "a brilliant synthesizer"; Paul Michael Garrett, a social work theorist who's decidedly less a fan of Bowlby, calls him a "collator," which is honestly a pretty sick burn coming from an academic.)

Bowlby had always been willing to turn his attention to whatever research might bolster his views and reputation. In the WHO report that first earned him international attention, he'd drawn only on the experts and studies that supported what he already believed—that mothers were at the center of a child's emotional health, and probably to blame if anything went wrong. Bowlby had responded to criticisms of that work by collaborating with scientists like Lorenz and Harlow, whose studies of mothering in animals seemed to bear out his beliefs. But throughout the fifties and sixties, Bowlby faced increasing criticism from psychologists and others who found his reliance on studies of ducks and monkeys to make arguments about human mothers and children unconvincing.

And as Harlow's research evolved, Bowlby faced a further problem: the monkeys raised by those perfect cloth mothers, though they'd seemed totally healthy, became deeply disturbed in adulthood. They couldn't socialize with other monkeys and wouldn't mate; when they were artificially inseminated, those "motherless monkeys," as Harlow came to call them, were neglectful or outright abusive. Perhaps those perfect, constantly available cloth mothers, who had no thoughts in their heads to take them away from their babies, weren't so perfect after all.

Even worse, for Bowlby's purposes, Harlow's later research further undermined the importance of the mother. Though Harlow's lab had started the monkey research focusing on mothers, subsequent studies showed that if you had to choose between isolating a baby monkey with a perfectly adoring cloth mother and depriving the baby of a mother but giving it access to other same-age monkeys for play, the baby with companions turned out better. In other words, peers can produce a socially and psychologically normal monkey, even without a mother. Bowlby handled these challenging findings from Harlow's monkeys the same way he handled most criticism of his work: by simply ignoring it, which turns out to work much better than you might guess.

Ainsworth's Strange Situation research had a kind of double advantage for Bowlby, then, particularly after animals stopped serving as convenient proof. Her research, with its formal protocol and quantifiable, replicable results, looked like the kind of science psychology was increasingly coming to expect. And Ainsworth personally was more amenable to the kind of deference Bowlby seems to have required of his research partners. Even as her academic reputation increased, she was willing to position herself as the junior partner. Writing about their partnership while both Bowlby and Ainsworth were still alive, Robert Karen noted the surprising lack of jealousy and competitiveness between them. He attributed the success of their longstanding relationship not to Ainsworth's innovative research methods or her intellectual prowess, but to her "supportive femininity."

Despite this portrayal of Ainsworth as "supportive" and

deferential, her accomplishments, particularly in a time when women faced many additional obstacles to their professional advancement, suggest a level of ambition that's largely gone unnoticed.

Ainsworth was the oldest of three girls, born to college-educated parents who believed in the value of higher education for their daughters, in a time when both of those things were unusual. But in many ways, her parents' vision for their daughters' lives was fairly conventional: they should get a college degree, work for a little while, but then get married, have babies, and stay home. "That plan worked perfectly for my younger sisters, but it didn't work for me," Ainsworth remarked.

Ainsworth had entered college at sixteen and earned her PhD in 1939, when she was just twenty-six. On graduating, she was determined to stay in Toronto, and when her advisor put her up for a job at Queens University in Kingston, Ontario, she deliberately flubbed it, downplaying her skills and abilities. Despite that, she was still offered the job, though the offer was retracted after the Senate of Queens University refused to hire a woman. She'd later insist this was the only form of sex discrimination she faced in her career. Despite the fact that pay in the Canadian Women's Army Corps was four-fifths of a man's wage, she called that "the reverse of sex discrimination," because she'd been promoted from second lieutenant to major within a year. One thing that goes unspoken in the conversation around Ainsworth and motherhood and gender is that, while she was an ambitious and successful woman, she was certainly not, even by the standards of her time, a feminist.

Ainsworth was hired in Toronto as a staff member, and when World War II began and most of the men in the department enlisted, jobs opened up, and she became a lecturer. In 1942,

Ainsworth joined the Canadian Women's Army Corps, and after the war, she worked for a time in the Canadian Department of Veterans Affairs, before returning to the University of Toronto as an assistant professor and the co-director of a research study with her former advisor.

In that research group, she met her husband, Leonard Ainsworth, a veteran who was returning to school for his graduate work. They married in 1950, and they decided that, since it would be "uncomfortable" for Len to be a student in the program where Ainsworth was on faculty, they would move to London, where Len had been accepted into a doctoral program at University College London. This is the part that always stops my heart a little: Ainsworth resigned from a tenure-track position in a city she'd never wanted to leave, in a time when it was legal to refuse a woman employment simply because she was a woman, and moved across the Atlantic, with no job in sight, rather than risk her new husband experiencing a bit of discomfort. Ainsworth wouldn't have another tenure-track job until 1958, after she'd moved continents two more times to support her husband's career.

This pattern—the couple prioritizing Len's interests and career—would persist through the rest of their marriage. When Len finished his PhD in London, he decided he was interested in working in Africa. Despite Ainsworth's concerns that such a move would make reentering academia in the US or Canada more difficult, they went to Uganda, where Len was hired as a research psychologist in the East African Institute of Social Research in Kampala, and Ainsworth was again on the hunt for a new position. Inspired by her work at the Tavistock Clinic in London, Ainsworth hoped to carry out observational research on mothers and children, but securing funding for such work in Uganda on such short notice proved difficult. The director of the institute where Len had been hired "scraped together," as Ainsworth later put it, enough funding for Ainsworth and a translator to begin a study in the villages around Kampala. The one directive attached to those funds was that there be "an anthropological component to the study."

In the Uganda study, Ainsworth visited twenty-six Ugandan households to observe the care of twenty-eight infants for their first fifteen months. (There were two pairs of twins in the study.) Based on her observations, Ainsworth categorized the children, using labels that slightly predated the Strange Situation protocol, as secure-attached, insecure-attached, and non-attached. Ainsworth focused on the mother-infant dyad, which her mentor Bowlby insisted was the essential unit, and she paid little attention to the broader context of childcare practices in the Ugandan villages where she carried out her study. Though her work was meant to be "anthropological," she did not, as a trained anthropologist would, learn the language, study family relationships or the local economy, or learn anything about each village's foods or history or celebrations. She watched the mothers, and she watched the babies. She observed shared care from older siblings and other family members, but she did not take shared caregiving into account when she analyzed children's attachments. Instead, she insisted, it was the quality of the mother's care that mattered most.

These findings foreshadow the way Ainsworth would write about mothers and babies for the rest of her career. According to Ainsworth, even mothers who gave their infants the constant care they believed they needed but didn't like it, didn't feel the right way about it, could still produce insecurely attached infants. Mothers who enjoyed breastfeeding, Ainsworth found, were more likely to produce securely attached infants. (And how do you measure enjoyment? Do you have to like it all the time, even when you've picked up the baby for the third time in an hour, even when your own dinner is getting cold, even after you'd just dropped into sleep?) Ainsworth assessed what she called "maternal sensitivity" in part based on interviews with mothers; those who were "excellent informants" and provided rich, specific details about their infants were seen as more sensitive. But this approach values a very particular idea of motherhood, one that focuses on what the mother can *say* about her child, as if the mother makes the baby hers through words.

For Ainsworth, it wasn't enough for a mother to be technically proficient. She had to *feel* the right way as she cared for her child. And she had to express those feelings in a way that would be intelligible to Ainsworth, a white woman with only a glancing familiarity with their culture. For Ainsworth, the good mother wouldn't just feed and care for her baby. She had to give the baby her whole heart as well.

Ainsworth clearly valued the opportunity to observe mothers and children in their own homes, which was a marked contrast to the laboratory research she'd conduct through most of the rest of her career. However, the way she talked about the Uganda study throughout her career makes it clear that, while she might have believed she was doing fieldwork, she had never been trained in the methods or theoretical frameworks of anthropology, which insists on careful observation; rich, detailed field notes; and a thoughtful consideration of the observer's own subjectivity and how the observer may be influencing what she sees. Ainsworth, in contrast, insisted that "despite all the language and other difficulties, I am convinced that it is easier to be objective when viewing another society." In other words, Ainsworth seems to have believed that she could drop into those Ugandan women's homes with the barest knowledge of their language or their culture and see straight through to the truth about their lives.

When they decided to leave Uganda after two years, it turned out to be just as tricky as Ainsworth had suspected for them to find jobs back in North America. Because her husband was less established in the field, she remarked, they focused on finding employment for him, and so they moved to Baltimore, where Len became a forensic psychologist. (This feels like bonkers logic to me, since Ainsworth's professional network would seem to be an asset in the job search, but even across the decades, I can feel Len bristling at the prospect of becoming the trailing spouse, hired into a lesser role at a university somewhere as a favor to his more accomplished wife.)

With their arrival in Baltimore, Ainsworth again began casting about for jobs, and after meeting with the chairman of the department of psychology at Johns Hopkins, she was offered a single evening class, which she "snapped up." She was ultimately offered a role as a lecturer—the same role she'd occupied years earlier, immediately after finishing her PhD—in a job that was "patched up" and consisted of evening teaching and clinical work at a hospital. She wouldn't be tenured until 1958, eight years after she left the University of Toronto to support her husband's graduate studies abroad. They divorced in 1960, something Ainsworth described as a "personal disaster" but insisted was not related to conflict over their careers.

Ainsworth's career trajectory bears a kind of spooky resemblance to the academic fates of Harlow's two wives, both of whom had to leave academic positions at the University of Wisconsin because of the university's nepotism rule. The University of Toronto didn't have a similar rule, and apparently there

wasn't much social censure there, either, against dating or marrying your graduate students. But where Harlow had thrived
at Wisconsin during and after both marriages, Ainsworth, like
Harlow's wives, paid the price for her marriage. This pattern
bears out for the other women in Ainsworth's PhD cohort. The
seven men in that group were all married, and they stayed married and raised children. Of the six women, in contrast, only
one had an enduring marriage; for the others, of those who did
marry, "their careers took off" only after they divorced. It seems
the best thing, for a woman with serious academic ambitions,
would be to never marry; failing that, divorce can provide a
boost. Many things have changed since Ainsworth's marriage
and divorce, but it remains true that women married to men,
even when they outearn their husbands, spend hours more each
week on childcare and housework, and those hours contribute
to the persistence of the gender wage gap. Divorce remains, for
many women, one way to finally get their husband to contribute
equally, even if it's by court order.

"This One Is a Charmer"

Ainsworth can be counted among the women whose careers
flourished only after divorce. Shortly after Ainsworth secured
her lectureship at Johns Hopkins, she began a yearlong observational study of mothers and babies that came to be known as
the Baltimore Study. Ainsworth and the researchers who've followed her argue that this yearlong observational study of mothers and babies in their homes was what gave credibility to all
the Strange Situation laboratory research that followed. As one
attachment theory proponent put it, the Baltimore Study is the

"small base" on which the "skyscraper of research and theoretical conclusions in attachment theory" is built.

But here's the thing about building a skyscraper: you'd better be certain its base is sturdy. And in this case, the skyscraper of Strange Situation research is all perched atop a remarkably precarious foundation.

In the Baltimore Study, Ainsworth and three assistants observed twenty-six mother-infant pairs in three-week intervals from when the babies were three weeks old to just past their first birthdays. Attachment theorists often applaud the amount of time spent with the mother-infant pairs during this study: eighteen four-hour-long visits, with a total of about seventy-two hours of observation for each pair. During these visits, the researcher looked for interaction patterns between mother and infant. Some mothers were seen as highly attuned to their infants' needs, with playful, responsive relationships observed. In other cases, the researcher determined that the mother was unable to match her infant's needs; for example, the researchers observed babies who choked and spit up while the mother persisted in trying to feed them.

We're supposed to admire those researchers' rigor, all those hours they spent in armchairs and couches, carefully observing the mothers and their babies, hoping to unlock the mystery in a mother's care that would set her baby on the right path. But I can't help but think about those new mothers, with a scientist sitting in their living room, watching them and marking down their flaws. Did any of them ever think to take the baby for a moment and give that mother a break? Or did they just add another tick on their clipboard each time the baby cried and the mother couldn't comfort her?

When that initial yearlong study ended, twenty-three of those mother-infant pairs came into the lab for the first Strange Situation. Ainsworth correlated behavior during the Strange Situation to behavior they'd observed in the babies at home with their mothers, resulting in the three groups—securely attached, anxious, and avoidant—at the heart of attachment styles research.

But wait: *This* is the real-world foundation for all of attachment styles research, just twenty-three mother-infant pairs? Even proponents of attachment theory note that this is hardly an exhaustive sample for an entire field to base its claims on. Ainsworth, near the end of her life, lamented that the Strange Situation had become such a central tool in attachment research and said she wished instead that researchers would return to doing fieldwork. "I have been quite disappointed that so many attachment researchers have gone on to do research with the Strange Situation rather than looking at what happens in the home or in other natural settings," she said in an interview. When asked why she thought the Strange Situation had become so popular, Ainsworth pointed to the "'publish or perish' realities of academic life!" While it could be difficult to get funding for fieldwork, which was time-consuming to carry out and harder to publish, laboratory studies could zip right along, speeding grad students' progress toward graduation and faculty members' path to tenure and promotion. But there's no reason to think the speed and convenience of a research method correlates to anything about what it reveals about the world.

• • •

It's actually not surprising at all that the painstaking, time-consuming work of observing families in their natural environment wasn't replicated. Real ethnographic research is slow and necessarily small in scale. This is particularly true if you actually take the care, which Ainsworth did not, to train your team to ensure that everyone's making the same kinds of observations and to record and code their field notes in a timely manner. It turns out that the lack of consistency across Ainsworth and her three assistants is only one of the methodological issues with the Baltimore Study.

One of the major shortcomings of Ainsworth's initial work in Baltimore has to do with her sampling. There are lots of ways of doing sampling for qualitative studies like Ainsworth's. I was taught, in my research methods seminars, that you had to have a deliberate procedure for recruiting participants. You can aim to select a group that's roughly representative of some larger population, or you can employ what's called a "snowball sampling" method where you ask each participant if they have other people they'd recommend for the study. What you can't do is more or less what Ainsworth did: pick people at random, and then claim that your results reveal something about the population as a whole. The mother-baby pairs in Ainsworth's study aren't really representative of anything, though the findings from those studies are the basis of big claims about all mothers and babies in general. They're certainly not representative of Baltimore at the time: though the city was getting poorer and Blacker, Ainsworth didn't want to have to deal with tricky confounding factors like race or class, so her participants were exclusively middle-class white women. And her research subjects aren't even representative of the population of middle-class white women in Baltimore in the 1960s—the sampling is more random even than that. The families in Ainsworth's Baltimore home studies were recruited through pediatricians, who recommended women they found *interesting* in one way or another. Ainsworth credited this method—taking recommendations from pediatricians based on remarks like "this one is a charmer, that one puzzles me, I wonder how motherhood will work out for this one"—for the "diversity" of their group, but any of the qualitative researchers I've known would call that haphazard sampling at best.

Moreover, the study was designed with assumptions about mothers and babies baked right into it. The researchers went at all times of day to see the mothers doing different activities—except, notably, in the evening, when the fathers would be home. Ainsworth described this as a limitation of the research, that they hadn't observed fathers with their children. But that's not a limitation; it's called research design. Much as she had in Uganda, Ainsworth decided before the study even began that the mothers were the only ones worth watching, so that's what she and her assistants did. If you've already decided that the mother-infant bond is the only one that matters, if you design your research study to observe only that—it's not surprising that that's what you find.

Beyond the design of the study, there are also serious questions about the quality of observations made by Ainsworth and her assistants. Each observer visited individually and made notes, but Ainsworth's focus on the observers using ordinary language to describe what they'd seen meant that the same language might be used to describe different behavior in different settings. Ainsworth rarely attempted to assess the reliability of these observations, only occasionally making the visits alongside her assistants. She seems to have supervised her assistants quite loosely, if at all, and one of the three, a woman named Barbara Wittig, did not even write up her notes until six months after her visits. Ainsworth acknowledged this later in a letter to Bowlby, nervously asserting that, despite this gap between observation and recording, the reports still had "freshness and vividness (and, as far as I can judge, reliability)." Though how would you assess the reliability of such an account, when you weren't there in the first place and the researcher who was didn't write it up for months after the fact?

The original records from the Baltimore Study reveal even more troubling issues with the research, according to historian of science Marga Vicedo, who viewed those records in the archives. Although proponents of Strange Situation research have long presented the study as a model of careful observational research, Vicedo's analysis of the original records shows that in many cases, the accounts were influenced by observers' judgments of the mothers and tension between the observer and the mother. The reports also vary significantly in the quality of detail, as well as their adherence to the directive to take notes every five minutes. In total, Vicedo argues, these reports "cannot be considered trustworthy scientific reports." All of attachment styles research is perched on top of these imprecise records of a narrow, haphazardly selected group of white women from midcentury Baltimore. The next time you're inclined to worry if sending your baby to daycare will doom him to a life of insecure attachment or wonder if your mother's occasional inattention in your childhood turned you into an avoidant mess, remember that those labels are undergirded with all the scientific precision of a middle-schooler's science fair project.

Reading about Ainsworth's casual approach to observation and fieldwork, I'm struck by the contrast with the women I knew in graduate school doing qualitative and ethnographic research. They didn't just sit in someone's living room and make random notes when they saw something of interest, then score those women months later on the basis of their memories. I was always awed by the rigor of those research projects. They developed interview protocols and sampling methods. They thought about their own positionality as researchers and considered how their research subjects might see them and how that might influence the information they gathered. They learned, some of them, entire new languages so they could conduct research in their subjects' native language. They transcribed interviews and coded their findings. Based on those studies, they made fascinating nuanced claims about what literacy meant in the particular immigrant communities they studied, how people with aphasia developed strategies for communicating when it was hard to produce language, how literacy moves people across borders. That's the promise and the potential of social science research methods.

But that kind of research is serious work. It's not only about the time spent in observation, but what you're looking at and how you make sense of it, the claims you're willing to make based on what you've learned.

In the absence of that kind of rigor, at a certain point—and I'd say Ainsworth's Baltimore Study and all the Strange Situation and attachment theory research that rests on that precarious base is well past it—it's not science anymore. It's just vibes.

Pumping and Problem-Solving

In my time at Wisconsin, I'd shared a series of windowless offices with four or five other graduate students. In those cinder block rooms, we were privy to each other's despair over seminar papers and frustration with dissertation advisors who were slow to respond to drafts or harsh in their eventual feedback.

We overheard each other's conferences with students. We knew who heated up soup for lunch, who ate peanut butter and jelly every day, who subsisted on the Pop-Tarts from the sixth-floor vending machine. Even by my diminished expectations of privacy, after months unlatching my bra to nurse at restaurants and friends' homes, it seemed obvious that if I was going back to campus for full days, I'd need a different space to pump.

When I inquired about pumping space, the English department admin handed me a set of keys for the sixth-floor women's lounge. I headed down to the room she had described, lanyard in hand. It was off the women's room, and I'd seen it before, when the room had been left unlocked. It had a long black lounge chair in it, the kind of synthetic leather that abounds in office parks and public universities. The lounge wasn't technically a bathroom, but it shared a door with one. You'd be able to hear the toilets flush as you pumped. Grad school had trained me to ask for little and be grateful for anything I got, though, so I didn't protest the bathroom-adjacent pumping space when I was given those keys. But I lucked out: the keys didn't work, and I returned to the office to explain sheepishly to the admin that I couldn't get the room unlocked and I was really going to need to pump soon. She looked at me again, paused, and handed me another key: a faculty office on the seventh floor, by some miracle empty for the semester. The office had windows that overlooked the concrete patio heading into the building. I'd have decent lighting, an outlet, and, most importantly, a door that locked. It was the nicest office I'd have in all my years in grad school, procured by dint of my lactating boobs and a no-nonsense admin who turned out to be, I'd learn later, a new grandmother.

I'd had a small stash of milk in the basement freezer, but I knew we'd need more once the baby was at daycare three days a week. When I was getting ready to return to campus, I ramped up my pumping again.

When I'd first started pumping, a few weeks after Penn's birth, I'd go into our guest room and shut the door behind me, as if I were doing something slightly inappropriate. My husband had been there for the birth, but I didn't want him to see me with my nipples stretched and gooey and distended in the flange of the pump. Two or three times a day, in those early months, I'd tuck myself away in the corner of the bedroom, and I'd diligently pour the milk from bottles into freezer bags that I'd label with the date. Once the fall semester had started, though, I mostly gave up on pumping. The babysitter was only at our house for two or three hours at a time, so I could feed the baby right before I left, and the frozen milk was there for emergencies.

When I returned to pumping that winter, though, something was wrong. I'd sit down with the pump, sit bored through its whomping, and look down to find a few dribs at the bottom of the bottle. Ten minutes later, sometimes an ounce or two, sometimes just a film: not nearly enough to feed a baby for three days a week.

I went to the natural baby store where I'd taken prenatal yoga to get help with my pump. As she connected the pump to a machine that would test its strength, the woman behind the counter mused, "Wouldn't it be nice if you didn't have to go back to work? If we lived in a civilized country where women could get six months or a year at home with their babies?" As she spoke, a little bubble of panic rose up in my chest: Surely there was no way this kind-eyed woman could make me stay home, could she? The thought—six more months at home with the baby, six more months away from my work while everyone I knew sped past me—filled me with anxiety. I knew parents who relished their time at home with their babies, and I'd certainly support longer paid leave and job protections to make that possible for anyone who wanted it, but I knew myself well enough by then to know that an extended maternity leave was not for me. I was desperate for those hours of work each week, the days on campus when I could transform back into a mind and not just an achy, nursing body. Pumping was part of how I'd pay for that time.

I tried everything. I bought different-size flanges, both larger and smaller, because nipple size could impact how your pump worked, but I had no idea if my nipples' problem was being too big or too little. I ate oatmeal and made barley water and ordered fenugreek supplements, which the internet said I'd be able to tell were working when my underarms smelled slightly of maple syrup. I looked at pictures of the baby on my phone while I pumped, I made recordings of his cry and listened to those, too. I tried, as every internet expert urged, to *just relax*.

Instead, that winter, as I pumped, I got angrier and angrier. I started pumping in the living room, but only after my husband had gone upstairs for the night. Carrying the pump and all its parts up and down the stairs was one more exhausting task at the end of the day, so I'd sit on the brown couch where I'd nursed the baby for hours when he was brand-new, and when twenty minutes would produce an ounce or two in each bottle, I'd fill with rage. One night, after pumping for fifteen minutes and producing just a few drops, I growled and closed my fist around the bottles. The flange flipped off my nipples, and a few drops of milk squirted out, wasted on the upholstery. Another night I was so angry I bit the bottle, and after that, whenever that bottle went through the rotation, I could see the ridges left by my teeth, and I felt ashamed of that, too. Ashamed that my body wouldn't work the way I wanted it to; disgusted by little floppy boobs, nipples like stretched taffy in the flange; angry and lonely on the couch by myself, failing at the thing nature had designed me to do.

There was an obvious answer to this problem, but it took me so long to get there. I'd sworn that I wouldn't use formula. Months before, when I was pregnant, I'd been talking with another grad student, also pregnant, after a meeting on campus, about our plans to breastfeed. Though I'd never, before having my own newborn, fed a baby a bottle of anything, I'd learned the "breast is best" lesson well and felt viscerally repelled by the idea of filling my all-natural baby with formula. I stood on the parking deck before we got into my car and threw up my hands. "I don't even know what's in that stuff!" I proclaimed. I'd been so certain about so many things before I became a mother, so quick to judge others, and myself.

That spring semester, I carried the pump in its nondescript black tote to and from campus, I shut the blinds and hooked myself up to the machine, I stored my paltry stash in the little cooler compartment, all the while feeling like failing farm equipment.

"Never Miss an Opportunity to Hold a Baby"

In a striking contrast to the scholarship on her male peers, Ainsworth's childlessness is frequently mentioned. You have to read deeply on Bowlby to learn that, while he was traveling around Europe and spending a sabbatical year at Stanford to gather evidence to support his argument that what a child needs most is the constant attention of a single caregiver, he had four young children at home. Harlow's lack of interest in his own children is never counted as a strike against his public image as an advocate for the wonders of maternal love. A woman, however, who devotes her career to the study of mothers and children, but who has no babies of her own risks being seen as unnatural (Didn't she want children?) or hard-hearted (If she didn't want children, what business does she have studying them?). Much of the scholarship on Ainsworth seems attuned to this potentially perilous intersection of her biography and her research, and it's frequently suggested that she made up for not having children of her own by taking a motherly position toward the graduate students she mentored. One attachment theorist calls her "the matriarch" of "a close-knit family of attachment researchers and theorists." "She never had babies of her own," one of her former students, clinical psychologist Robert Marvin, mused, "but in a very real sense, she has sons and daughters throughout the field of psychology who love her very much."

At first, I wonder if this sometimes-pitying description of Ainsworth as a maternal figure for her students is just the condescending foolishness of men who can't imagine a woman's life complete without children. But Ainsworth herself, it turns out, frequently spoke about "the children I had vainly longed for." She'd married relatively late for her generation, at thirty-seven, and her one pregnancy ended in miscarriage. Late in her life, Ainsworth told a journalist that "quite a lot of my wanting my own child played into my life work." She spent her career like that: watching mothers and their babies, and, she said, "If I was encouraged at all, I'd pick up a baby, hold it, bounce it on my lap and display affection."

But if she'd had the children she wanted, would she have had a career? Ainsworth, like Bowlby, was skeptical of working motherhood, though she had the grace to be a little gentler in how she phrased it. (Which is to say, really, that she'd been socialized as a woman.) "It's very hard to become a sensitively responsive mother if you're away from your child ten hours a day," she argued. "Had I myself had the children I longed for, I like to believe I could have arrived at some satisfactory combination of mothering and a career," but, she notes, there is no "universal, easy, ready-made solution." I wonder, though: Had she been able to have those children, and particularly if she'd become a mother after beginning her career and becoming enmeshed in her research, would she have seen the tension between work and motherhood differently? Would she have found it so easy to pick up the baby and put down her work, as she insists good mothers should do?

Milk and Mimosas

All that time I was pumping and struggling and trying to figure out why I was failing at the thing that, by definition, made me a mammal, it took another mother to help me see things differently.

When I was pregnant, I'd become friends with Emily, whose husband happened to also be a grad student in English, and our babies were born a few weeks apart. In February, Emily invited me and a bunch of department-adjacent moms to her place for a party she was calling "Milk and Mimosas."

Mike and Emily lived in a set of condos along Lake Mendota. The complex, a small one-story set of buildings, was more modern than anything else on our side of town. Nearly every other graduate student I knew lived in a complex of charming but aging apartments. Emily and Mike's place, in contrast, felt like a genuine grown-up place, still polished by the New York life they'd lived before moving to the Midwest. They had a clean-lined modern high chair positioned in the front room by the kitchen counter, a clear tarp taped to the floor to protect the carpet when baby Prudence threw food on the ground.

I sat in the sunroom among the mothers. At six months, my baby was among the youngest there. Dina's baby, whom I'd admired as a wide-eyed three-month-old when Penn was brand new, was beginning to crawl. Another baby pulled up on the coffee table.

I stepped away from the mothers for a moment. I walked into the kitchen to get more coffee. Emily was standing on the other side of the kitchen counter, and a canister of formula was on the counter beside her. I was shocked. Emily and I had done prenatal yoga together. She'd visited me when the babies were weeks old and we spent an afternoon talking in my living room as the babies cooed and nursed and slept.

Emily must have seen me looking at the formula. "I started supplementing," she said. "Pumping at work was so hard, I'd always be having to reschedule a meeting, and it took so much time out of my workday." Her office didn't have enough privacy for pumping, she told me, so every time she'd needed to pump, she'd have to stop her work and go across the office to the little lactation suite. It wasn't worth the hassle, she decided.

A few weeks before, at Penn's six-month well-baby visit, I'd told our doctor I was having trouble pumping. "It's so hard to produce enough for the pump, and it's really stressful, since he's in daycare now," I explained. "If we're going to start supplementing with formula"—and here I paused nervously—"is there anything you recommend?"

Almost without pausing, my doctor responded, "It doesn't really matter. They're basically all the same."

I'd heard her advocate enough times for breastfeeding to fill in the rest for myself: *They're basically all poison. If you're going to feed your baby that stuff, I'm not going to help you pick.*

Or maybe, I can see now, that's not what she meant at all. Maybe that's just what I, in my guilt and self-judgment, heard.

Emily's reasons for supplementing—for giving her baby the formula that had made me recoil—were so entirely reasonable. I looked at her in her kitchen that day, the kind of composed, loving mother I so wanted to be. She was giving her daughter formula, and they were both still fine. If I didn't judge her for that, why should I judge myself?

All the Rage

In that first winter as parents, we fell into a regular rhythm. Three mornings a week Smith drove the baby to daycare and I took the bus to campus. I learned which bus would get me home on time to drive to daycare pickup, the exact minute I had to walk out the door of my office to get to the bus stop on time. I washed the pump parts and the bottles and the Tupperware containers of baby food while the baby banged in his high chair. And what was Smith doing, while I was scrubbing and multitasking and tensing my whole body in preparation for the baby's inevitable fussing? He was *working*. Some nights, when the baby waved a broccoli spear and sang a little song, or when he chewed on the yogurt spoon and burbled, I was so content I wanted to stay in that blue kitchen forever. And other nights the rage rolled off me in waves. Could he feel it upstairs? I don't know.

I was the one making basically no money, and I was also the flexible one. Of course, I'd made myself that way. I'd learn, years later, listening to Darcy Lockman describe the research that shaped her book *All the Rage: Mothers, Fathers, and the Myth of Equal Partnership*, that mothers partnered with men inevitably describe their careers as more flexible. And there was joy in that: swim lessons in the freezing pool at the Y, where the baby splashed and pawed the rubber duckies, afternoons with Angela and baby Phoebe, or Ana and Lauren. But also: my wild, panicky typing in the locker room while the baby was at the Y's Child Watch, because there was never enough time for teaching and research and writing; the feeling that never quite subsided that, all through my department and across the country, students were racing ahead of me. In those months, I was writing, I was sending out abstracts for academic conferences, I was applying for department jobs for the fall, I was sending my poetry manuscript out to contests. I was tracking my running, tracking my weight.

When my period came back, I was recording that, too, one eye on my fertility. Every time I placed another stack of outgrown baby clothes in the basement in a labeled Rubbermaid, I thought about having another baby to wear them. With all I'd learned, I was certain, with the next baby I could really do everything right.

. . .

Late in his life, Bowlby argued that the findings of attachment theory, and particularly the vital necessity for mothers to stay home with their children, should lead to "a huge scientific and civic campaign akin to the one that abolished polio." But the thing that abolished polio was the vaccine, a positive intervention in the prevention of disease. Bowlby argued instead for a negative: the closure of daycare centers, the diminishment of women's work as not just a silly waste of time but a danger to humanity.

The underlying problem is how we've defined what it means to be a good mother. A good mother, according to our mythology, would hate leaving her baby's care to anyone else and would use daycare only if absolutely necessary. But this mythology is wrapped up in class and patriarchy—a woman who has a bread-winning husband to support her while she's caring for their children is a stay-at-home mother, while the words we've got for a single mother relying on state support are much less kind.

But there are better ways of thinking about the relationship between mothering and work. Black mothers, as the sociologist Patricia Hill Collins's research shows, have often thought of working and providing for their families as just something a good mother does. Rather than working and feeling bad about it, she argues, Black mothers have seen work as a central way to be a good mother. For Mexican women who've migrated to the US to earn money to support children at home, researcher Gabrielle Oliveira has found, wage-earning is also an essential part of what it means to be a good mother. And the mothers she studied went to extraordinary lengths to remain engaged in their children's lives, even from thousands of miles away, calling to check in on grades and homework and contacting their children's schools when necessary. This combination of work and mothering is made possible, of course, by childcare, and Collins documents the way that Black mothers have relied on the support of "othermothers," the network of sisters, aunts, cousins, grandmothers, and neighbors who provide care. These cooperative, community-based approaches to mothering can help to free us all.

If we are really taking the lessons of attachment research seriously, there are clear policy implications. If we took Bowlby and Ainsworth at their word and believed a child needs his mother's uninterrupted attention for at least the first three years, we'd have paid parental leave and universal healthcare so that mothers and babies could be cared for from pregnancy through to the postpartum period.

But it's cheaper, and more politically popular, to just place all those impossible contradictory expectations on women and call them weak when they can't heft that weight. From Bowlby to the present day, mothers have been sent a much simpler, and much meaner, message: go back home, and like it.

· 5 ·

You Know More than You Think

The first thing I did when I got pregnant—before I was pregnant, actually—was turn to books. I read about prenatal nutrition, the glowy magic of early motherhood, the tricks French women used to get their babies to sleep through the night and lose the baby weight to stay sexy for their husbands. I studied books on sleep and read about first foods and baby-led weaning, just to get ahead. Each week of my pregnancy, I consulted the handbook I'd been given by my doctor that recounted what the baby was doing now and how I could best care for him. The answer, it seemed, was always by forgoing any pleasures: alcohol, obviously, but also rare meat, soft cheese, most fish (for fear of mercury) but not all (the omega-3s were essential for baby's developing brain), soft-cooked eggs, any sauce that might contain a raw egg, skiing and biking (you might fall), and even the spin classes—on a stationary bike!—that I'd gone to on campus with friends and loved. At every turn, there was so much to learn, and a whole roster of experts eager to teach me what I needed to know.

Motherhood seemed—especially early motherhood, with its dizzying array of decisions (Breast or bottle? Nanny or daycare? Stroller or wrap?)—to be primarily a research project. Emily Oster's *Expecting Better* wasn't out yet, but the promise of data-driven parenting was in the air. I read a column in *Slate* by a science journalist who parsed all the recent studies to figure out why your four-year-old had suddenly turned clingy and what to do about it, or if it's really true that sleep training would irreparably harm your baby's brain. The sleep website I loved best— mostly because it made me feel least like a failure—promised its advice was all supported by the most recent research.

I was, obviously, by my training and my temperament, more predisposed to this research endeavor than most. But now— especially on social media—you don't have to seek out parenting advice for it to find you. If you so much as think about a baby, you'll find your feed flooded with parenting coaches, natural mamas, trad wives, accounts of #honestmotherhood, and more. Women are spending more time researching the right way to do everything, and there's always more to read and more people willing to tell you what to do, or why what you've been doing is wrong.

In an interview with *The New York Times*, one mom, Kristin Gallant, described the pressure parents feel to always be parenting the best way, and suggested that research plays a central role in finding that perfect parenting style. "When we have two hours after bedtime, we are still researching the best things for them," she said, adding, "You'll never do it perfectly, so then you're chasing more." Of course, this "chasing more" works out well for self-proclaimed parenting experts, who often profit by ramping up parents' anxiety, then promising to alleviate those worries by teaching a seven-step tantrum strategy or offering scripts you can memorize to handle any situation. Gallant herself is one of the creators of Big Little Feelings, a wildly popular Instagram account that's expanded to offer online parenting courses on topics like "Winning the Toddler Stage," a "game-changer and life-saver," for only $99. But who are we winning against? Our toddlers? The other moms at the playground who aren't yet so enlightened? And what if, instead of using those precious post-bedtime hours for studying up on expert techniques to help us optimize our kids, we used those hours for ourselves? If we've got two hours to scroll Instagram or watch a parenting webinar, that's time we could use instead to talk to a friend, read a book, have sex, get caught up on our own sleep.

It's easy for me to be coolly skeptical now, but honestly I'm really lucky that the parenting advice industry hadn't yet taken Instagram by storm when my first baby was born. I was already buried under piles of sleep books and baby nutrition guides, but there is, fortunately, a limited amount of time even the most intrepid mother-researcher can spend reading a print parenting manual. I would have been a prime target for the #relatable parenting guidance that abounds online today. I would have been not just drinking the Kool-Aid but eagerly pulling up a chair and buying the whole pitcher, for a low, low price when it comes bundled with the courses that promise to solve all your problems.

This degree of research, this seeking out of expertise has become an expected part of the labor of parenthood—and it's work that falls, like so much else, disproportionately on mothers.

Dr. Spock, "Confidence Man"

Before Emily Oster and Dr. Becky and Big Little Feelings, before even *What to Expect*, there was Dr. Spock. Today, Spock is best remembered for the encouraging words that open his *Common Sense Book of Baby and Child Care*: "Trust yourself. You know more than you think you do." Those oft-repeated sentences contributed to Spock's reputation as a kindly, warm figure, available to provide advice but ultimately handing the mantle of expert back to the mother. The words that follow, however, are less famous and muddy the narrative: "Bringing up your child won't be a complicated job, if you take it easy, trust your own instincts, and follow the directions that your doctor gives you." Spock reassured the mothers he addressed that they already had the essential knowledge and skills to raise their children, but he also constantly referred them, in his book and in the columns he wrote for women's magazines, back to their pediatricians. What a bind: take it easy, trust your instincts, *and* follow your doctor's directions. One historian famously described Spock as a "confidence man," zippily assuring mothers that they already have everything they need while simultaneously undercutting that self-confidence. This is a throughline from Spock to today's parenting gurus: they're warm and encouraging, but you often feel just a little more on edge after you watch their latest video, a little more unsure of your parenting, and, not coincidentally, more likely to open up your wallet to pay for more guidance so you can finally do it right.

Spock's strict New England childhood was a far cry from the warm, reassuring advice that would make him famous. Born in 1903, in New Haven, Connecticut, Spock was the oldest of six children. His mother loved babies, and his sister Hiddy, only a year younger than him, remembered well into adulthood how the whole household filled with excitement before each birth. Their mother, Mildred, would allow the children to come look at the baby clothes and the bassinet, and each new baby, Hiddy remembered, was "king or queen of the house." But beyond babyhood, Spock's mother was stern, an adherent of L. Emmett Holt, whose book *The Care and Feeding of Children* was then a popular manual for child-rearing. Following Holt's ideas, Mildred established firm rules for her children in all areas of life: they slept, year-round, on an unheated second-story porch and ate an almost entirely vegetarian diet. Even bananas were deemed too rich for a child's "delicate constitution." Hiddy remembered that with her friends, Mildred could be witty and charming and warm, but at home, she was a strict disciplinarian, with high and unwavering expectations for her children. Spock's *Baby and Child Care*, with its insistence that a mother set aside rigid schedules for sleep and feeding and instead learn her baby's rhythms and moods, was a direct rebuttal to the experts who'd guided his mother's parenting style. This change in style, combined with a growing market of new mothers hungry for guidance, paid off for Spock: in its first year, Spock's book sold more copies than Holt's had in nearly forty years.

Like his father before him, Spock went to Yale, though his mother insisted he live at home in his first year. Spock was a middling student, and he finally found his place on campus when he joined the crew team in his second year. He competed on the Yale men's eight-member team that won a gold medal rowing in the Seine at the Paris Olympics, then came home to finish his degree and start medical school at Yale, where a C average was, in those days, enough to get you in. He married Jane Cheney, who'd been a student at Bryn Mawr when they met, and he transferred to Columbia's medical school so the two could move to New York—and, it seems, get a bit of distance from his mother, who remained enmeshed in his life. Mildred held a deep suspicion of women who went to college and who, she believed, thought too highly of themselves, but she eventually warmed to

Jane, once it was clear the marriage was inevitable. At Columbia, Spock did much better academically, and he graduated in 1929 at the top of his class.

In those early years in New York, when Spock was in medical school and then residency, earning nearly nothing, it was Jane's work that supported the young couple. Jane got a job as a research assistant at Presbyterian Hospital, where the doctor she assisted was investigating the connection between psychological and physical problems. At her boss's encouragement, Jane began psychoanalysis. She'd remain in therapy for the rest of her life. Though Spock would become famous in part for introducing American parents to psychoanalytic ideas through his book, it was actually Jane who first brought Freud into their home.

Faced with the challenge of building a practice in pediatrics during the Depression, Spock looked for ways to distinguish himself. He hoped that, since the public was developing an interest in psychology as presented in newspapers and popular magazines, having additional training in psychiatrics might help attract new families to his practice. He began training in psychiatry at Cornell's Payne Whitney Psychiatric Clinic in the New York Hospital, but found that he had little success with his challenging young patients. He then embarked on training in psychoanalysis, attending seminars at the New York Psychoanalytic Institute twice a week and entering analysis himself. This mixture of pediatrics and psychoanalysis proved appealing to a clientele of academics and intellectuals, and Spock would come to count Margaret Mead's daughter, Mary Catherine, among his patients.

Even with this psychoanalytic training, which would eventually reshape Spock's perspective on parenting and inform the advice he gave mothers, the lessons from Spock's own upbringing and the scientific wisdom of the day proved hard to shake when he and Jane became parents. When their first son, Michael, was born in 1933, Spock insisted Jane adhere to a strict feeding schedule and leave the baby to cry alone in his crib between feedings, lest he be spoiled by too much love. Jane said later that she hated it, that she stood outside her son's nursery wracked with worry until the clock ticked to the time she was allowed to go in and soothe him.

Spock was still a relatively inexperienced physician when, in 1938, an editor at Doubleday, intrigued by the idea of a Manhattan pediatrician drawing on Freud to treat his young patients, approached him about writing a book. Spock turned that offer down, certain he didn't yet know enough to be an authoritative guide for new parents. Five years later, an editor from Pocket Books approached him, offering the odd assurance that, since it would only cost twenty-five cents, the book didn't have to be very good. This time, Spock felt ready, and, with Jane's urging, signed a contract to write what would become *The Common Sense Book of Baby and Child Care*.

Spock had never learned to type, so each night after their son Michael went to sleep, Jane and Spock worked on the book together, Spock pacing the room and dictating while Jane sat at the typewriter. She fact-checked and contributed her own practical knowledge, adding information like how many diapers a new mother should buy, and ensuring the book maintained a conversational tone. When Spock entered the Navy in 1944, at the tail end of World War II, when the military desperately needed qualified physicians, they continued working together on the book, with Spock calling every night to dictate to Jane. At first, he was in Bethesda, but then he was assigned to a hospital in California, pushing their late-night phone calls even later. By then,

Jane was also the mother of a newborn, their son John, born in 1944, shortly after Spock enlisted in the Navy, but she continued taking dictation over the phone long into the night until the book was finished. Though the book was dedicated to her, she'd later insist she should have been listed as a co-author. It would take until 1976, with the publication of the fourth edition of the book, for Jane to get anything more than cursory credit for her work. The dedication to that edition began "To Jane with Gratitude and Love," noting that "the book couldn't have been what it is without her."

Though the book was published with little fanfare, it quickly became far more successful than Spock or his publisher had dreamed. Within the first year, it sold not only the 10,000 copies they'd hoped for but more than 750,000. The book was released simultaneously in a hardcover edition meant to impress Spock's physician colleagues and a paperback edition aimed at parents, priced cheaply enough (with the twenty-five-cent price tag the editor had originally promised!) that anyone could get a copy. That part of the strategy worked especially well: many of the mothers who wrote to Spock when he had columns for *Ladies' Home Journal* and *Redbook* reported owning multiple copies of his book, keeping them in the kitchen and the bathroom and the glove compartment of their cars, so they'd never have to be more than an arm's length away from Spock's reassuring voice. Spock would quickly come to regret one part of this publishing strategy. In his eagerness to get his book into as many hands as possible, he'd agreed to accept no advance and a very low royalty rate to help keep the cost of the book low. Even as his book flew off the shelves, he found that he wasn't making enough money for his family to continue to live in New York, prompting a series of moves, first to the Mayo Clinic in Minnesota, then to

Pittsburgh, then to Cleveland. Its author's (or perhaps more appropriately authors') financial woes aside, by the time of Spock's death in 1998, the book had sold fifty million copies and been translated into forty-one languages. For much of the second half of the twentieth century, Spock's book outsold everything but the Bible.

Spock's *Baby and Child Care* cast a long shadow across popular culture as well. Two First Ladies, Mamie Eisenhower and Jackie Kennedy, said publicly that they raised their children by his methods. When Lucy and Ricky were trying to decide whether to send little Ricky to nursery school in a 1955 episode of *I Love Lucy*, it was Spock's book that they consulted. Spock used his fame to draw attention to political causes. He was the first celebrity to march with Dr. King. He was indicted in 1968 for conspiring to aid resistance to the draft, and he was arrested countless times in the following decades for his activism against war and nuclear weapons.

Though Spock had more progressive politics than, say, Bowlby, who it's easy to imagine, in his pressed suit and red suspenders, yelling at hippies to go get a job, Spock and his legacy are complicated. I'd long imagined Spock as a simple, kindly figure, Mr. Rogers in a Brooks Brothers suit, but he's a considerably more complex character, and the messages he gave American mothers across his decades as a public figure are contradictory. Spock seems to have genuinely thought of himself as a friend to mothers. His first readers, the mothers of the baby boom generation, many of them marrying younger and having more children than their own mothers, and, because of increasing geographic mobility and suburbanization, raising those children away from their own extended families, were desperate for advice. Spock was there for them—but, poor royalty rates aside, he also gained enormously from being the first and best-known expert in a burgeoning industry designed to guide these women through motherhood. Spock played a central role in the decades-long movement toward expanding the domain of a mother's responsibility while continually suggesting that she's not fully up to the job. As one scholar put it, "The Spockian mother has 'common sense,' though perhaps not in excess since she must consult a 500-page book to rear her child." Spock encouraged women to enjoy their children, telling mothers, "Don't be afraid to relax, be agreeable." But on top of that encouragement to relax, he layered complete responsibility for their children's emotional health and well-being. While previous childcare manuals had focused primarily on nutrition and hygiene, Spock's book entrusted mothers with responsibility for their child's psychological health as well, work that amounted, as one historian put it, to "an emotional workday superimposed on the mother's physical workday." It was no longer enough to just keep your baby clean and safe and growing: a good mother would also attend to her child's particular personality, his minute-by-minute happiness, and she knew that if she failed him in babyhood, there would be lifelong consequences. This combination of urgency about the stakes of every choice in parenting, combined with the promise of a straightforward fix turns out, of course, to be an excellent marketing strategy. No wonder he sold so many copies!

There's a key difference, though, between Spock's time and ours. The advice available to new mothers now is nearly infinite. When it was time for Penn to start solid foods, I had a whole array of philosophies and guidebooks at my fingertips, from the old-school choice of rice cereal and purees to the hipper baby-led weaning approach. And now there are entire Instagram accounts devoted to recipes for baby food and tricks to get your toddlers to eat veggies, the vast majority of which come with a heavy dose of diet culture and anxiety in the comments. But when those midcentury mothers consulted Spock, they had a single finite and authoritative resource. It seems almost sweet now, the certainty that every time they looked up colic or diaper rash or constipation, they'd find the same concise advice. It's such a contrast to the ever-expanding realm of parenting advice now and the pressure to have the best guidance, based on the most up-to-date data. Spock's book was designed with short sections and an index so that it could quickly be skimmed. As he revised each edition, Spock aimed to keep the book compact enough that a mother could always hold the book in one hand and the baby in the other.

And this image of the baby in one hand and the book in the other feels to me like the real legacy of Spock: the belief that, for any parenting challenge, there's an answer, and there's an expert who can guide us to the right solution. Those women frantically flipping through Spock at breakfast or bedtime, trying to figure out what to feed their baby or how to get him to go to sleep, echo so neatly my own frenzied googling of every baby problem, the countless nights I spent in the dark searching "make baby sleep" or endless daytime stretches on the couch, nursing the baby while reading tips about how to wean him off the pacifier or what would be the best choice for first foods. Spock is an essential part of how we got here—believing that motherhood is a simple matter of love and instincts, but also wanting to double-check and cross-reference every decision with the best available data from trusted experts.

"Pennsylvania for Some Homemade Pumpkin Pie"

A few months earlier, as winter arrived in Wisconsin, we'd driven through Chicago and across Indiana and Ohio, ten hours across the flat, featureless highways of the Midwest before arriving at my mom's house for Christmas. It was by far the longest trip we'd taken so far with the baby, but it was fine. He slept. He looked around. Smith and I took turns driving, and the baby was content in the back seat. And when we arrived, we were greeted by my mom and stepdad and my sister, who'd flown in from North Carolina: three whole extra adults, all eager to hold and love the baby. My mom placed the pink-and-green quilt she'd been given at her baby shower when she was pregnant with me on top of the living room carpet, and the baby rolled around happily while we relaxed on the couch. He was wearing Christmas jammies, and he grabbed the Santa face printed on each foot. When my oldest stepsister had her first baby, my mom had transformed their finished basement into babyland, outfitting one of the bedrooms with a crib and light-blocking shades and placing a changing table in the hallway. My mom, who'd always proclaimed that she never liked any babies besides her own, had turned into a doting grandmother, and she wanted to make sure it was easy for those grandchildren to come home to visit.

That night, after the baby was tucked into his crib, I sat at the kitchen table with my mom. White noise from the baby's room whooshed through the monitor. I leaned forward to tell my mom something I'd thought about so often since the baby's birth: how much my grandmother, my mother's mother, would have loved him. She'd been gone for years by then, but having a baby of my own brought her back to me. She could be a difficult woman, exacting and precise, hard to please. But I knew this baby, this son especially, would have softened her. I could see it so clearly: the baby cradled in her arms, one perfectly manicured hand behind his head, the other on his chest. The genuine joy on her face as she looked down at my son.

"Oh, she would," my mother answered, but something else passed across her face, too.

My grandmother wasn't a cookie-baking, big-hug kind of grandmother. Even thinking of her now, I sit up straighter, her dinner table etiquette lessons ever-present, years after her passing. She always knew the right thing to say or wear or do, and she was quick to correct her daughters and her granddaughters.

My mother was raised very differently than she'd raised me. When she talks about her childhood, it always sounds like *Leave It to Beaver*: a mother at home, with her hair done and a cocktail ready for her husband when he returns from the office, children who should be seen and not heard. "We were just objects to them," my mother has often said. She knew how she was supposed to look and behave, and her parents made it clear that their daughters' accomplishments were proof of their own parenting. Now that I have my own child, I've been thinking about how we learn to parent, how so often we seem to be aiming to heal the hurts of our own childhoods.

"But how did you learn to do things differently?" I asked that night at the kitchen table. "How did you figure out what kind of mother you wanted to be?"

"Oh, I read a lot of books," my mother said. For her, as it would be for me, this was the obvious solution: experts and advice. "And I just loved you so much," she added, reaching across the table to squeeze my hand.

Birthing the Baby Boom

I don't know how my grandmother learned to mother. Her generation was the first to embrace Spock and his gentler, less schedule-obsessed approach to motherhood. At a distance, the broad sketches of her life line up with the trends that contributed to Spock's popularity: she'd gone to college and worked before getting married; once she did marry, she moved away from home. She became a mother young. She must have needed guidance. I can imagine her, a young mother in the years right after the first *Common Sense Book of Baby and Child Care* was published, picking up a copy at Tops along with her groceries.

In my earliest memories of my grandmother, she's newly retired from a job in social services, driving around town in her Oldsmobile delivering Meals on Wheels and volunteering at the hospital once a week. For years, almost into her eighties, she drove "elderly friends" to doctors' appointments and hosted friends for cocktails before dinner at the Bradford Club. She'd been a housewife and a skilled hostess, had spent summers with her daughters at the country club and at her family's house on Chautauqua Lake. In my memory, she's always wearing the wrap skirts she had custom-made at the dressmaker's in town, paired with wedge espadrilles. She never once wore pants until her late seventies when she was recovering from knee surgery. She hated the way "Grandma" sounded, and even "Grandmother" made her feel too old, so her granddaughters called her by her first name, though we were allowed the slight softening—Jeannie instead of Jeanne—that no one else would have gotten away with. She was smart and fearsome, the prototypical eldest daughter, long before that was an internet joke.

It did not occur to me until well into adulthood that she

might have once wanted a different kind of life. When I was a girl, motherhood seemed so much like the natural state for women that I never wondered if she might have thought herself destined for something else.

My grandmother married young, but, I eventually learned, that hadn't been her original plan. She'd wanted to be, like her father, the president of a bank. Jeannie went to college and majored in economics, but someone—I don't know if she ever told me who; it may have just been obvious, accepted wisdom—set her straight: the best she'd be able to do was executive assistant. If she was lucky, she'd be secretary to the president. For a time, she thought that maybe that would do, and she went to Katharine Gibbs in Manhattan for secretarial school, but she didn't stay in New York City. She went home to Allegany, the small town in New York where she'd been raised, and worked in her father's bank until she married. My grandmother gave birth four times in less than six years. Her first daughter, with whom I share a name, died when she was a few days old, and when my mother, her youngest daughter, was born, the doctor gave Jeannie a hysterectomy along with a caesarean. My grandmother wouldn't have dared question a doctor, so none of us know what led to the hysterectomy. She would have been just thirty then. She was a devout Catholic, the second oldest of six, but if she'd hoped for more children, that chance was taken from her. Her sisters both had five children.

When my grandmother married in 1948, she was only twenty-three, but she'd been to college and she'd had a job. From the late forties through the fifties, the average age for motherhood and marriage fell, the fertility rate soared, and divorce rates dipped. My grandfather, a veteran who went to law school and bought a home after his military service, was exactly the kind of person postwar policy was designed to benefit; my grandmother, equally smart and certainly more driven, faced culture and policy created to keep her in the home. Parenting advice at the time was aimed directly at women like her, not only because she was of the class likely to have the education and disposable income to consume it, but also because many feared that once women had had a taste of public life, they might not be content to simply stay home with their children. Redefining motherhood as something requiring expertise became another way to lure women like my grandmother into pursuing it. Books like Spock's, which positioned motherhood as both easy and pleasurable and also a quasi-professional endeavor, where your performance could be improved through education and research, were one attempt at convincing those women that motherhood was worthy of their educations and their ambition. Of course, this advice was also carried on the currents of racism and classism. As many at the time were worried that educated white women would stop having babies, one of the goals of that era's parenting discourse was to draw them into the project of raising the next generation.

I don't know which set of experts my grandmother might have turned to as she raised her daughters. Self-assured as she always was, it's hard to imagine her asking anyone for help. I do know that my grandmother believed in fresh air for children and, like Spock's mother, would place her babies on the back porch for their naps. Among the handful of black-and-white family photos from our mothers' childhoods that a cousin shared with me, I find a photograph of my aunt as a blond bowl-cut toddler, standing in a playpen in the middle of the dining room. She doesn't look upset, but she's not being entertained, either.

I hear echoes of that older, sterner generation of advice in a story my mother frequently tells, about her parents' first visit to see me after my birth. My grandparents sat stiffly on the couch, certainly smoking then, even with a newborn in the house, and my mother held me, wiggling in a whale-printed navy onesie, and cooed at me. Even as a newborn I had tufts of bright red hair, a color my father had to go back two generations, to his own grandmother, to explain. My birth had been difficult. I'd been delivered with forceps, my collarbone broken as the doctor scooped me out. My mother is too prim and proper to give details, but now that I've given birth myself, I have some sense of the injury that kind of delivery causes. During that visit my mother would have still been bleeding, still stitched together in her most sensitive parts. She nursed me in those early weeks, and her breasts would have been heavy with milk.

My grandfather sat in the living room and watched my mother as she cuddled and whispered to her new baby. "Well," he remarked, in tart disapproval, "I never saw anyone so happy with what they got."

. . .

In that same packet of photos, I found one photograph of my grandfather as a young man, slim and dark-haired in a button-down shirt. He's holding a baby, I'd guess my oldest aunt, and looking down at her like he can't quite figure out where she's come from. When I showed the picture to my mother, she paused for a moment before musing, "I've never seen my father with a baby before."

My own father was an every-other-weekend dad. After my parents' divorce, he was a voice on the phone—after 8:00 P.M., when long distance was cheaper—or a body on the interstate, traveling to meet us. He was always late, so huge chunks of my childhood were spent waiting for him at the McDonald's perched on top of Cresson Mountain halfway between our house in Pittsburgh and his in Central Pennsylvania. We'd listen to NPR and when the radio grew staticky across the Alleghenies, I'd ask question after question, simply to hear him talk. The shelves in his house were layered two books deep, volumes of American history and political theory. I'm sure that nowhere among those stacks of books was anything approaching parenting advice.

And no wonder, really: for all the millions of pounds of print parenting manuals and Instagram accounts and podcasts aimed at training and supporting mothers, the material directed at men is thin and largely uninspiring. It seems that every man I know is just trying to do better than his own father, that every man I know is trying, as he enters fatherhood, to imagine himself into an unmapped terrain. They know, in many cases, what they don't want to be, and simply by talking to their kids and hugging them and helping with dinner and bedtime, most of them are doing better than their own fathers. When I was pregnant, Smith read *The Birth Partner*, but the books and websites I consulted frantically for advice on everything from swaddling to sleep training to first foods didn't interest him, and they weren't really aimed at him, either. The presumed audience was always the mother, the comments full of women griping and sharing tips and asking for further help. Though this is beginning to change, there's no clear destination for men looking to become better fathers. At the same time as the parenting advice industry has exhausted and overwhelmed mothers, it's shortchanged fathers.

This gap in advice—with mothers presumed to be the ones doing the research and then passing on their findings to their presumably less-able husbands—also makes it harder to imagine parenting as a partnership. It probably goes without saying that, for a long time, mainstream parenting advice has been determinedly heteronormative, focusing on straight couples, and this is often deeply alienating for queer couples, single parents, or anyone else whose family doesn't fit that narrow norm. I remember a friend telling me how, during her own labor and delivery class, the doula leading the session on postpartum recovery made a joke about dads needing to be patient about waiting for sex, then looked nervously at my friend and her wife.

Before my son was born, I had an image of motherhood, shaped by my own excellent mother, by the books and blogs I'd spent years consuming, by the women whose work I'd been observing my whole life. I was surrounded by models of what it meant to be a mother. The expectations were too high, and they were contradictory and exhausting, but they were there. It took me years to realize that I didn't really know what a dad was for, what a man might do, day to day, in the raising of a child. It didn't occur to me to wonder. I hadn't, while pregnant, thought much about how my husband might fit into my new life as a mother, and when I was struggling, it felt like motherhood was something that was happening to me, not an experience we might share. Once we had a baby, I realized I couldn't actually do it all alone, but I didn't know what it might look like to share the work.

Spock's Change of Heart

When Spock approached the stage for the National Women's Political Caucus, whose endorsement he was hoping to secure for his third-party bid for the 1972 presidential race, he must have thought he had a lock on the women's vote. Spock had long thought himself well loved by women—didn't they buy his books, didn't they send him adoring letters? So when the crowd booed him, and one woman walked out in protest, he was shocked. Gloria Steinem tried to explain the crowd's reaction to him, telling him that "you are considered a symbol of male oppression—just like Freud."

In truth, Spock shouldn't have been quite so shocked. By the early seventies, he was facing backlash from all sides. When his liberal politics became more widely known, he'd left the conservative *Ladies' Home Journal*, where he'd written a column for nearly a decade, and moved to *Redbook*; despite his anti-war stance and other progressive positions, he wasn't far left enough for some, and feminists critiqued his focus on motherhood in a time when women were fighting for lives outside the home. In *The Feminine Mystique*, Betty Friedan had blamed Spock for the "Freudian mania" in American culture, arguing that the psychoanalytic ideas Spock had dispersed into American homes made mothers all-important—and easy targets when anything went wrong with a child. Like many of the midcentury men of motherhood, Spock's reputation began to waver when second-wave feminists looked carefully at what he'd been saying about women and families. Unlike most of those men, though, he tried to listen.

Following that disastrous 1971 speech, Spock attempted to repent. He apologized for his sexism and vowed to remove stereotypical depictions of women from his books. However, he managed to miss his critics' larger point, focusing on grammar over substance, as if what feminists were really upset about was that the baby was always referred to as "he." He seems to have been unable to shake the deep ideas about gender roles that were really at the heart of the feminist critique of his work. Later that same year, Spock wrote an essay in *The New York Times Magazine* titled "Male Chauvinist Spock Recants—Well,

Almost." Despite his desire to be seen as a "friend to women," as he put it, he couldn't help doubling down on the Freudian ideas about gender that had drawn feminists' ire. In that article, he insisted yet again that little girls experienced penis envy and that boys' accomplishments in arts and engineering were driven by the realization that they could not grow a baby. (And not by decades of culture of policy designed to make it easier for men to achieve public acclaim, typically supported by a wife behind the scenes.)

It should be no surprise that Spock was being critiqued by and responding to white feminists; Black women already knew he wasn't really writing for them. In 1971, the same year Spock was booed by the feminists of the National Women's Political Caucus, a *New York Times* article called for "A Dr. Spock for Black Mothers." In that article, Joanne Dann presented African American mothers who, when questioned about the significance of Spock for their mothering, responded, "He's for rich kids. He can't help my children." Their response reveals the way that Dr. Spock's bestselling advice rested on certain assumed truths about caretaking, time, and labor—truths that predominantly applied to households occupied by middle- and upper-middle-class white families.

In spite of his support of Dr. King, it doesn't seem to have occurred to Spock that he might be attentive to the ways his advice might be received by women of color; however, he did try to listen to the mothers who sent him their feedback, updating his books with each new edition and responding to questions in his magazine columns and speeches. Women wrote to him about the impossibility of actually following his guidance, particularly that it just wasn't possible to be totally attentive to multiple children, that his approach was exhausting and overwhelming—and he responded, across his magazine columns and the many editions of his book, by changing his advice.

The most significant changes to *Baby and Child Care* were in how Spock addressed the role of fathers and how he talked about mothers who worked. From the beginning, Spock's books had positioned the mother as centrally in charge of the care of her child; the 1946 edition notes that mothers might want to seek help from neighbors or relatives, but they remained the primary caregiver. It's assumed that the mother is at home all day and wouldn't want to burden her husband, who's outside in the world providing for his family. By 1976, however, Spock revised the opening of the book, asserting that "the father's responsibility is as great as the mother's."

However, this ends up being only a superficial revision; while the opening articulates a more equal balance of labor between mother and father, the text of the rest of the book remains basically unchanged. The illustrations also confirm the idea that the mother is the primary caregiver of the child—and the only one who's really competent at caregiving. A father is featured in only two illustrations in the book, and in only one of these is he engaged in a caregiving task. In this illustration, he is attempting to feed a young child, but he clearly doesn't know what he's doing—the baby is sitting on the edge of a table and leaning over to look at a puppy, while the father holds out a spoon and looks confused. A new mother seeing that illustration might not take it as encouragement to hand the care of her child over to her husband. The 1985 edition, catching up to the wave of women entering the workforce and staying there after becoming mothers, included more information aimed at mothers who work, such as a section on breastfeeding for working mothers. Spock later said that "every time a mother told me something even slightly different from my previous concepts, I revised my ideas accordingly."

In this, Spock stands in stark contrast with the other men of his era, who doled out parenting advice and shouted women down if they disagreed. Bowlby, asked about the compatibility of attachment theory with working motherhood, dismissed both women's contribution to the workforce and the value of daycare centers in one fell swoop: "women go out to work and make some fiddly little bit of gadgetry which has no particular social value, and children are looked after in indifferent nurseries." Harlow, interviewed by a young psychologist named Carol Tavris for *Psychology Today* in 1971, began their conversation by asserting, "If you don't believe that God created women to be mothers and essentially nothing else, let me prove it to you." Since Harlow's own work doesn't actually claim that only women can mother, much less assert anything about God's plan, it's hard to say if he actually believed any of it, or if he was just annoyed at having his research called into question by feminists and an increasing number of female graduate students asking him difficult questions when he traveled to give lectures. Spock was also traveling during those years, touring the country to protest war and nuclear weapons, and everywhere he went, he said, "the women followed me, yelled and hollered until I really woke up." Of course, his change of heart wasn't immediate; he also noted that it took him five years to really understand what all those feminists were talking about.

One prominent feminist was eventually persuaded by Spock's reinvention: Gloria Steinem, who listed him in *Ms.* magazine's tenth-anniversary edition in 1982 as a hero of the women's movement. "He's proven to be a long-distance runner, who responded to criticism constructively and never lost his ideals," she wrote.

As much as I admire Steinem, whose catchphrase about how a fish needs a bicycle was a refrain throughout my mother's self-proclaimed flaming feminist years, her assessment of Spock feels like the kind of easy praise often heaped on men who've done the barest minimum.

Spock's changes to *Baby and Child Care*, however superficial, also coincided with big changes in his personal life. His long marriage to Jane had come to an end, and by the time the 1976 edition was published, they'd divorced and Spock was seriously involved with Mary Morgan, a woman forty years his junior who would become his second wife. The 1976 edition also included the first detailed acknowledgment of Jane's contributions, a four-paragraph note that dutifully stipulated that "it was Jane who spent hundreds of hours on the last-minute revision and indexing . . . The book couldn't have been what it is without her." In a 1976 *Newsweek* article announcing their divorce, Jane suggested that this belated acknowledgment, late as it was, was still insufficient: "I did an awful lot more than he put in the dedication."

It's hard to know how to feel about this late turn in Spock's biography. He seems to have been genuinely very happy with Mary Morgan, and his marriage to Jane had long been troubled. More difficult to figure out is the gap between Spock's guidance for parents and his actual parenting of his own sons. When social conservatives in the late sixties and onward began accusing Spock of leading the way toward a permissive parenting style that had ruined a generation of children, Spock's son Mike spoke up publicly: as a father, Spock was often cold and harsh, not at all the warm figure he'd appeared to be in his advice columns and during his public lectures. A review of Spock's biography in *The Washington Post* captured this contradiction in the headline

"Public vs. Private: Dr. Spock, Mr. Hyde." Spock himself was under no illusion about his shortcomings as a father. Late in his life, he told an interviewer that his guidance for fathers could best be seen "through my writing, not my example." All the same, it's a sad kind of irony that Spock guided generations of women into raising their children with empathy and love, and seems to have found it so deeply difficult to apply those same principles in his own home. In this way, if not others, Spock's story is similar to so many of the other men of motherhood.

From Dr. Spock to Dr. Becky

When my grandmother died, she'd been sick on and off for a year or more, and every time my mother called, I braced myself for the final bad news. My grandmother and I didn't talk much in that last year. I was far away, in my new life in graduate school, and it was hard to think of things to tell her that she'd approve of or understand. When I'd last seen her, at Christmas, I'd been laughing with Smith and my sister on the couch, and from across the room she'd scolded us as if we were children, as if our happiness were inappropriate. I wonder now if she was in pain, if she knew the end was approaching. But also: she had an exceedingly narrow definition of appropriate behavior.

She died on my twenty-eighth birthday, a day I spent on campus teaching and then taking an evening poetry workshop, so I learned of her passing only when I finally checked my voicemail as I walked out into the October dusk. I rode the bus home in the dark, and when I got there, a card was waiting for me, my grandmother's writing a bit shaky but still legible, still unmistakably hers. Addressing that card must have been one of the last things she did, correct until the end. I opened the card and burst into ugly tears. "I'm just so mad at her," I sobbed. "She could be so mean." Smith scrambled to book a flight for her funeral using the frequent-flier miles we'd somehow saved. I could get there from Madison, a miracle, on two tiny planes via Cleveland, from our regional airport to an even smaller municipal one in my grandmother's small town perched at the top of the Allegheny National Forest in northern Pennsylvania.

She could be so judgmental, and she made herself hard to know. When that card arrived, it felt like the presence of a ghost.

At the funeral and the lunch after, surrounded by my aunts and cousins, I was reminded of the side of my grandmother I'd forgotten: how, when we visited, she'd warm the towels on the radiator so we'd be cozy getting out of the bath, how she'd buy Entenmann's coffee cake, a special treat, with its plasticky frosting and strip of raspberry jelly, for our breakfasts. How she loved the lottery and would buy us scratch-off tickets, once dashing from the parking lot back into the store three or four times in a row when my sister and I had a streak of small wins—$2 or a free ticket—that sent her rushing back to the counter to redeem our earnings. From her sisters, I heard stories of Jeanne in girlhood, how she loved golfing and the Buffalo Bills, how when she worked for her father, she'd spend her breaks smoking and flirting with the state troopers at the lunch counter across from the bank. Her youngest sister told me that Jeanne "didn't do anything that she didn't do well." If I was trapped by a parenting-advice complex that made me think and overthink every choice, that caused me to spend hours pondering nap schedules and bedtime routines, she wasn't, I don't think, beset by that kind of anxiety in her motherhood. Instead, she was a woman of considerable aptitude and ambition limited by a time that told her those traits were best put to use inside her home.

And now I wonder: How would she have told her own story, what would she have written, if she'd thought her life worth writing down? Mothers have so often written ourselves out of our own stories. Even the baby books report growth and milestones with a mother only seldom present. As if the baby did all that on their own.

When I was planning my wedding, I'd call my grandmother sometimes to chat about the flowers or the centerpieces or the bridesmaids' dresses. I thought the wedding would be safe conversational territory. But as often as not, she'd flip the topic, asking instead about how my graduate school applications were going, what program I was hoping to attend. I found it perplexing at the time, but now I wonder if she was telling me something: that she knew I'd do things in my life more important than getting married, that I might become something besides a wife.

When I think about us now, I see my grandmother, my mother, and myself as three points on a century-long arc of mothering. From Holt to Spock to the countless momfluencers and parenting gurus on Instagram, the voices have multiplied and the advice has only gotten more complex and more difficult to follow. That arc has progressed continually toward more research and more expertise applied ever more intensively to every area of children's lives. We know more than ever about evidence-backed methods for potty-training and which experts can help us learn how to get our kids to eat their vegetables—but each new piece of advice, each new voice telling us how to do it right, seems to only make us more anxious about our kids, and about ourselves.

6

Many Warm, Friendly People

For my first night away from the baby, I drove six hours south to Indianapolis with a friend for an academic conference, and after we'd checked in to our room, we went down to the bar in the lobby. I'd freshened my eyeliner and we chatted with the bartender, flirting a little. *No one here knows I'm a mom*, I thought, thrilled and a little disconcerted. *I could be anyone now. Does the baby know I'm gone? Does he know I'm coming home?*

That night in the hotel room, with the air conditioner thrumming and the single cocktail I'd had at the bar zipping through my veins, I slept poorly. I'd had the fantasy that I would go away for one night and would somehow, with no baby to wake me, emerge refreshed and recovered from the previous nine months of sleep deprivation. Instead, I woke to my phone's insistent beeping and dressed to go read my paper in a conference room before driving the six hours back home, where it turned out that while I had been tossing fitfully in hotel sheets, the baby had slept right through the night for the first time.

For weeks he'd been screeching and wriggling, moving from

something like a push-up into a kind of down dog, as he attempted to crawl. He'd push up to hands and knees and rock back and forth before falling down. He couldn't quite get his limbs coordinated, and sometimes I knelt on the floor beside him, trying to work out the necessary mechanics for myself.

When I came home from Indianapolis, he was on the hardwood floor in our living room, wearing a striped hoodie and brown fleece pants with a bear on the butt. I sat on the floor to greet him, and he crawled across the gap that separated us, screeching with glee at his ability to get himself where he wanted to go.

"It's All Anthropology"

Before she was, as *Time* named her in 1969, "Mother to the World," American anthropologist Margaret Mead was "the flapper of the South Seas," as newspapers breathlessly called her when reporting on her journey to Samoa in 1925 when she was twenty-three. Mead went to the South Pacific planning to immerse herself in a new culture and learn lessons about adolescence that she could bring back to America, but her work was also influenced by her perception that the people she was setting out to study were "primitive." She would write, in *Coming of Age in Samoa*, that anthropologists choose to study "quite simple peoples, primitive peoples, whose society has never attained the complexity of our own." As Samoans since then have rightly pointed out, it's hardly accurate to call a civilization that learned to navigate the Pacific Ocean by stars "primitive." Despite those limitations, Mead came back from her fieldwork with genuinely good ideas about parenting, most notably that children did better not in the locked box of the nuclear family but when cared for by a whole community.

As she told the story later, Mead's first plan had been to become the wife of a country pastor, with five kids and a big rambling house to which they'd welcome everyone from the village. When she married her first husband, Luther Cressman, she'd just graduated from Barnard, and they had a brief honeymoon in a New Hampshire cottage, where they slept in separate bedrooms because Mead was busily typing the research papers that were due when she began her graduate work, in the anthropology program at Columbia, in the fall. Despite the utterly conventional life Mead said she'd imagined for herself as a child, she was full of questions, and she traveled across the world in pursuit of answers. It's hard to imagine her following through on that initial plan to live quietly as someone's wife and, instead of work, fill the house with babies. It's perhaps even harder to picture Mead, who believed in free love and had affairs with both men and women throughout all three of her marriages, committing herself to the fidelity such a provincial life would presumably have required.

Before setting out for Samoa, Mead had a brief affair with another anthropologist, Edward Sapir, whom she met at a conference in Toronto. Sapir, two decades older than her and ahead of her in his career, had admired her research when she presented it. They met again in New York, checking in to the Hotel Pennsylvania under false names, when she was preparing to set out for Samoa. He insisted he was in love with her and begged her to divorce Cressman and marry him instead. Though he'd initially been enthralled by Mead's "brilliant mind," his real agenda soon became clear. He was a recent widower, and what he was really looking for was a wife to raise his children. Mead could so easily have chosen the seemingly easier path of abandoning her own career in favor of the security of marriage to an older man, already established in her field. She could have, like Peggy Harlow and so many academic women of their day, spent her life instead doing unpaid labor in the lab, adjacent to her own ambition.

Mead would not be that woman. Over Sapir's escalating objections, she continued her preparations for the long voyage to Samoa. Sapir wrote to Mead's mentors at Columbia, Franz Boas and Ruth Benedict, insisting that something must be done to prevent her from leaving. She was too frail, he argued, for such a trip. "The girl is going crazy," he scrawled in a note written on anthropology department letterhead, though from today's vantage point, it isn't Mead who was acting erratically. She wasn't the one using department resources and social capital to attempt to prevent a lover from leaving. Sapir found another woman to be his wife and stay home with his children. He'd continue disparaging Mead in public and private for the rest of his life.

Franz Boas, though he had not initially encouraged Mead or any of his female students to travel so far afield, seems not to have listened much to Sapir. Boas wrote the preface to *Coming of Age in Samoa* that helped catapult Mead to fame. He helped her get the job at the American Museum of Natural History that she'd hold, with intermittent breaks for research trips and war work, for most of her career. "I have had a curious experience in graduate work during the last few years," Boas once wrote to a colleague. "All my best students are women."

Another one of those excellent women students was the anthropologist Ruth Benedict, who'd recruited Mead into Columbia's anthropology program. Mead met Benedict in the fall of her senior year at Barnard, when Mead took an introductory course in anthropology. Benedict was Mead's teaching assistant, and across that semester, the two began spending time together, with Mead sometimes riding the bus with Benedict from Columbia to the Museum of Natural History and back to Columbia so they could continue talking. Benedict accompanied Mead on the first leg of her journey to Samoa, sharing a train car from New York until near the Grand Canyon, where Benedict would begin a summer of fieldwork. It was on that voyage that they became lovers. Mead's relationship with Benedict, by turns intimate and intellectual, would last until Benedict's early death in 1948.

When she left for Samoa, she wrote a letter to Cressman in which she promised, "I'll not leave you unless I find someone I love more," which she did in fairly short order, when she met her second husband, an anthropologist from New Zealand named Reo Fortune, on the boat ride home. She said later that she'd decided to divorce Cressman when a doctor told her a tipped uterus meant she'd be unable to have a baby. Since the quiet country life she'd imagined wouldn't be possible, she chose a different kind of life. Reo Fortune, her second husband, would make a terrible father, she thought, but a good partner in the field. Between the two of them, they could observe both men and women, dividing up areas to study, thereby learning the culture in a level of detail she couldn't achieve on her own. This was the same idea that had led Boas to recruit women into the graduate program at Columbia, believing that the emerging discipline of anthropology would need the insights of both women and men to earn its status as a science.

Boas was right about Mead, but Mead was wrong about Fortune. Her second husband turned out to be a difficult spouse and a less than ideal research partner, prone to jealousy and violence, and lacking Mead's passion for the work.

Against her doctor's advice, Mead decided to have a child. She had at least one miscarriage while married to Fortune, before meeting Gregory Bateson, who would become her third and final husband and the father of her child. Mead met Bateson, the Cambridge-educated son of a prominent biologist who'd coined the term *genetics*, while she was in New Guinea with Fortune, and the three spent several malarial weeks in a mosquito tent together. By the time the trip was over, Mead was determined to divorce Fortune and marry Bateson, who she believed would be a better father. After several more miscarriages, Mead finally gave birth to a daughter, Mary Catherine Bateson, in New York City on December 8, 1939. Bateson, who was abroad at the time, trying to contribute to the war effort in Britain, missed the birth. He wouldn't return to New York and meet his daughter for several more weeks.

But Mead wasn't alone in early motherhood. Throughout her life as a mother, inspired by the shared caregiving she'd observed in her fieldwork, she built a community around herself and her daughter. In fact, when she and Bateson had returned to New York from Bali when Mead was pregnant, they had no home of their own, and they didn't set one up. Instead, they stayed with friends, and when Mead and her newborn daughter, Catherine, left the hospital, they moved in with Mead's good friend from college, Marie Eichelberger, whom Catherine would come to know as Aunt Marie.

Mead's experience in the field influenced her choices throughout motherhood, beginning with the birth. Mead insisted, against the practice of the time, on having both the obstetrician and a pediatrician present, and she wanted to have her birth filmed, in part because she believed that the baby, in the first hour after birth, is "more clearly herself than she will ever be again for days or months." She was determined to breastfeed, and she wanted to keep the baby in the room with her at the hospital, decades before that became the norm.

Mead chose for her pediatrician a young doctor she referred to as "Ben Spock." She'd met him when they both attended lectures at the New York Psychoanalytic Institute, and Spock had been interested in Mead and Bateson's research on child development in New Guinea and Bali. Mead believed Spock's interest in psychoanalysis might mean he was more open to ideas about child-rearing that went against the norm. As it turned out, Mead's own ideas about parenting became an important influence on Spock's career and on the advice he doled out to women in his baby book.

Many of the ideas at the heart of Spock's advice to mothers, like following your baby's cues for feeding rather than sticking to a rigid schedule, came first from Mead, who'd observed on-demand breastfeeding for years in her anthropological fieldwork. He'd become "Dr. Spock" to millions when his first book was published seven years later, in 1946, but Mead's daughter, Catherine, is sometimes referred to as "Dr. Spock's first baby."

For Mead, the anthropologist's habit of close observation was not just a research method but her primary way of interacting with the world. As she said when she was profiled in the *New Yorker* in 1961, "The whole world is my field. It's all anthropology."

Mead and Bateson carried that anthropological approach into their daughter's childhood. They kept detailed records of everything Catherine did, and Catherine said later that her clearest memory of her father from her early childhood is of him standing with a Leica camera around his neck. At a time when so many parents were still following the rigid parenting manuals, whose advice had persuaded Spock himself to keep his first child to a strict feeding schedule and leave him to cry in between, Mead and Bateson were doing something radically different. Rather than getting their child to adhere to the schedule and rules an expert set out, they worked, through meticulous observation, to get to know their own child.

Years later, Catherine would speak of this habit of observation and recordkeeping as a core part of her family's culture. "In my family," she wrote, "we never simply live, we are always reflecting on our lives."

Anthropology Versus Attachment

Mead debated, in print and in person, the researchers studying attachment theory and maternal deprivation from the very beginning. She based her critiques on the cumulative years she'd spent observing caregiving in her fieldwork. Mead practiced participant observation, and when she was in the field, she learned the language and became immersed in each community. She attended births, held babies, played with children, and talked with old men. She worked tirelessly, those long months in the field, spending her days rotating through groups of women and children, her home often full of groups competing for her attention. She typed her field notes late into the night. Subsequent researchers and Samoans themselves have rightly criticized some aspects of her work, suggesting she did not understand Samoan culture deeply enough to accurately report on a subject as fraught as the sex lives of adolescent girls. Though her titillating claims about what Samoan girls were getting up to after dark may well be flawed, her observations of shared caregiving remain compelling. The caregiving Mead observed in the field shaped her own parenting and, even today, point the way to a gentler, more cooperative way of raising children.

Proponents of Ainsworth's research point out the hours she spent with those new mothers and their babies as proof of the depth of the observational work supporting the Strange Situation laboratory protocol. But those intermittent visits, and Ainsworth's method of dropping in on families in Ugandan villages for an hour or two, communicating through a translator then scooting off to the next village or back home to Kampala in her little Peugeot, quickly feel flimsy and insufficient in comparison with Mead's months-long total immersion in the community she studied.

While Ainsworth, in both Uganda and Baltimore, kept a narrow focus on mothers and babies, Mead had been trained to examine the whole culture. It's not enough, according to anthropologists, to observe a mother and baby alone in their home. You have to understand the whole community, anthropologists insisted, their language and economy, their folktales and their values, their history and their kinship networks. Mead went to Samoa hoping to learn lessons about girlhood and adolescence that could be applied to American culture. But she didn't set out already believing she knew what she would find. And she didn't think that being an outsider would give her a clearer look into the objective truth of others' lives. Rather, she set out to understand the culture on its own terms.

Ultimately, the difference between Mead on one hand and Ainsworth and Bowlby on the other is not just one of discipline and experimental methods, though those are important. Certainly, Mead's training in anthropology led her to attend to context, rather than isolating individual actions and moments. And in-depth fieldwork will yield a radically different perspective than a twenty-minute laboratory protocol or one-hour observations mediated by a translator. In the end, the difference is even more profound: it's not just what makes a good mother, or what a baby needs, but how we learn about the world, and what kind of evidence we think will lead us to the truth.

Mead tackled those topics directly when, from 1953 to 1956, she and Bowlby met yearly in Geneva as part of a WHO-convened study group, along with experts in child psychology, animal behavior, cultural anthropology, biology, psychoanalysis, and more. Mead loved these kinds of gatherings and believed that the lively debate and cross-disciplinary exchange of research they afforded was the best way to generate new insights. She described that study group as "my most rewarding intellectual experience of the post-war world." It's doubtful that Bowlby, who'd begun his 1950 WHO-sponsored research trip to speak with experts across Europe by blithely asserting that half the people he'd been tasked with meeting would be "pretty stupid," had a similarly open mind.

Though Mead really should have been seen as the senior scholar—she'd been internationally famous for decades, held a position as an assistant curator at the American Museum of Natural History, had a list of publications and awards that towered over Bowlby's—he seems to have simply refused to engage with her ideas. He cited Mead only once in his career, in a footnote in his 1969 book *Attachment*, and only there to insist again that she had misunderstood him and was wrong.

When the WHO decided to publish a new report considering critiques of Bowlby's *Maternal Care and Mental Health*, he decided he was too busy to engage with his critics. Instead, he enlisted Ainsworth to write on his behalf.

Ainsworth's article presents an even more expansive definition of maternal deprivation than Bowlby had initially proposed. While Bowlby had focused on mothers who failed their children by dying or going to work, Ainsworth argued that it was possible to deprive your children even while you were physically present. Distraction could also be a form of deprivation.

In fact, Ainsworth concluded, "deprivation occurring without physical separation can in fact be as pathogenic as deprivation occurring with separation." In other words: even if you're physically there every moment, if you're not 100 percent present, if you think of anything else or want anything else besides your baby, you're doing just as much harm as if you've abandoned your child entirely. As wild as that sounds, the idea is with us still: in the 2003 edition of *The Baby Book* by William and Martha Sears, the attachment parenting manual that influenced the "natural" mothering that surrounded me in Madison, they write about "the most common infection of the employed mother—*distancing between mother and child*. This occurs as a result of mothers having other thoughts than their children at work." Simply *thinking* of things beyond your child puts the bond at risk. Even today, our discomfort with mothers who seem not fully engaged with their children—mothers scrolling on their phones at the playground or pushing strollers with headphones in are often the subject of online disdain—continues.

Mead, on the other hand, offered a whole new way of looking at children and caregiving. While most contemporary experts argued that the nuclear family, with a mother as her child's primary caregiver, was both natural and ideal, Mead knew from her research and her own life that there are many ways to make a family. She argued that an exclusive mother-baby bond would, in most societies, actually be more dangerous for the infant, since it put the child at risk if the mother became ill or died or otherwise wasn't up to the task of caring for the child all on her own. While Bowlby insisted that nature and evolution had made mothers the ones best positioned to care for their babies, Mead made the practical point that you needed easy, consistent access to food, as well as birth control to space out children, to make that ostensibly natural way of mothering even possible, much less optimal.

Instead, Mead argued, children did best when cared for by "many warm, friendly people." While Harlow praised the eternally available cloth mother and Winnicott described the easy subsuming of a mother's entire self to meet her baby's needs, Mead's years of observing caregiving in Samoa and elsewhere had shown her another way. In the field, she'd seen siblings and extended family caring for children alongside the mother, and in her own life, she surrounded her daughter with a network of other children and loving adults. This kind of shared caregiving, which biologist E. O. Wilson called "alloparenting," is common across the animal kingdom and human communities alike. In his 1969 book *Attachment*, Bowlby used observations of four primate species in which the mother is the sole caregiver to argue that this is what nature intended for human families, too—but he conveniently ignored the primate species that engage in shared care. While attachment theorists have often pointed to hunter-gatherer or forager communities to make arguments about our evolutionary past, here, too, they've been selective in the cultures they cited. (And that's leaving aside the inherent racism of assuming that present-day communities are somehow closer to the past than the industrialized West is!) Much has been written about the !Kung people of southern Africa, a hunter-gatherer community whose practice of continually carrying their infants would put even the most devoted attachment parenting practitioner to shame. But, it turns out, the mother isn't the only person holding the baby. When researchers looked again, they found that, yes, the babies were only rarely put down, but it wasn't only the mother doing the carrying; other caregivers were holding the baby nearly a quarter of the time. And recent studies in anthropology have found that, in some communities, allomothers, or caregivers other than the mother, contribute nearly 50 percent of the care. Siblings and grandmothers are often important sources of support for mothers. It's too hard to say what's "natural" for something as complex and culturally dependent as parenting—but it seems clear that Bowlby's image of the adoring mother doing it all on her own is the outlier across the world.

Though he refused to cite her, it seems certain Mead's criticism of Bowlby rankled him. In fact, her criticism of his work spurred a disdain for anthropology as a whole such that, following that study group, he simply refused to collaborate with anyone in the field. When Harvard anthropologists Sarah and Robert Levine visited him in London, Bowlby assumed that, because they'd been researching shared caregiving in Nigeria, they were there to criticize him, and he rejected them out of hand. One attachment theory researcher notes that because Bowlby viewed anthropologists as "uninterested in the nuances of his work," he essentially rejected the discipline wholesale—though it's equally fair to say that Bowlby was uninterested in the nuances of anthropology, or any other field that might have challenged his long-held beliefs.

It's no surprise, really, that the man who wrote gleefully to his wife about his flourishing professional network while she stayed at home raising their four children and writing a book that would not be published in her lifetime, who'd characterized Ainsworth as his junior partner throughout their decades-long collaboration, would have been unable to hear the voice of a woman telling him he was wrong. After all, Bowlby had attended Cambridge during the decades in which women were permitted to enroll but would never be granted a degree, no matter how seriously they took their studies or how high they scored on their exams. Everything in his upbringing and his education had taught him that women's ideas simply did not merit attention.

What might attachment theory have become, had Bowlby been able to take seriously the evidence shared by Mead and others that, yes, a mother is important, but a child does best with the care of a whole community? I imagine a theory that would take seriously the deep love between a mother and her baby and also understand that that love grows best with the care of a whole community. Such a theory of caregiving would have consequences for culture and for policy. There's so much we might have dreamed and created within that framework—the kind of state-supported childcare and flexible work arrangements available in much of Europe, perhaps even the wilder utopian feminist dreams of thinkers like Charlotte Perkins Gilman, who saw the single-family home as a site of oppression and argued for the construction of the "feminist apartment hotel" where families would eat in a shared kitchen and nurses and teachers would care for the children so mothers could work. Instead of a broken marketplace of childcare that costs parents far too much and pays childcare workers far too little, we might have state-supported nurseries, as is the case in much of Europe. Instead of a school day that assumes a mother is waiting at home at three o'clock, we might have community centers where children could play together until both parents finish work. If we believed that raising healthy children was the role of the whole community, we'd see a greatly reduced gender wage gap, particularly since that gap grows ever wider when women become parents. If we understood that children needed a whole network of care, we'd stop shaming single mothers and instead examine the supports available for families in the whole community.

Instead, living in the long shadow of Bowlby, Ainsworth, and attachment theory, we're stuck with an image of motherhood that's as resilient as it is unattainable: the good mother who cares for her child single-handedly, who knows her child best, who is fiercely capable and tender and doesn't even mind. Her love for her children powers her devotion to them at the same time as it effaces any part of her that might want something different for herself. She's the most important person in the world to her baby, and because she's so important, she has to do it all alone.

A Baby at Diss Club

That spring, as the lakes unfroze and the enormous piles of dirty snow plowed into the corners of the Capitol Square began to melt, I was typing away at my dissertation. I taught intermediate composition Monday, Wednesday, and Friday at 9:55 A.M., and when the class ended, I pumped, then got back to what I thought of as my real work, the pile of words gradually accumulating into chapters of a dissertation. One or two days a week, I'd meet a friend in the library or at a coffee shop to write together. I'd seen students in the cohorts ahead of me pass their exams, then spend years and years seeming to wander around as they fiddled with a dissertation proposal and agonized over their chapters. I was determined to not slow down, to not get caught up in the perfectionism and self-doubt I'd seen capture other grad students, and I set an ambitious schedule for sending drafts to my advisor. I had my eye on the job market for the coming year, and if I finished two chapters that spring and another over the summer, I'd be ready.

To keep graduate students on track once they'd passed their exams, my department had started organizing something they called "diss club," in which a group of six or so dissertators would meet twice a month to share drafts, get feedback, and commiserate and encourage each other. Faculty members took turns hosting and were there largely to guide the discussion and give the "club" a kind of official imprimatur. We met in the comp/rhet area room, the kind of slightly grim academic office space where public universities put their humanities programs. The faculty offices overlooked Lake Mendota, but the area room was windowless, lined on one side with bookshelves full of old copies of scholarly journals, the shared mini fridge and microwave on the other, so that the room always smelled a bit like someone's lunch.

One Friday that diss club was scheduled to meet, daycare was closed, and though it was my turn to have my work discussed, I'd have to take the baby with me. (I know: The baby had another parent, a competent caregiver who was working from home. But I was the mother, the one with the flexible grad student schedule, and the baby felt like my job. Though I didn't know the word yet, I saw myself as the default parent, and I also didn't know that the caregiving patterns set in infancy— who feeds the baby, who knows his nap schedule and how to pack the diaper bag, who learns the tricks to keep the baby calm during a diaper change—can persist for years. Making parental leave available to non-birthing parents, and establishing policy and culture so that they can actually take it, has a dramatic impact in equalizing the work of caregiving well beyond infancy.)

I drove to campus and looped around and around looking for a parking spot after finding that the small garage below the building that housed the English department was full. I finally found one on Langdon, about a block away from the lakeside building that housed the English department. Because I wanted to seem jaunty, like mom-slash-dissertator was an easy role to inhabit, I hadn't brought the stroller, so I carried the baby in his car seat past the Memorial Union and up Park, then across the concrete plaza to the elevator, heaving the awkwardly swinging carrier from one arm to the other. By the time I pressed the button to call the elevator, I was sweaty and aching, not at all, as I'd imagined, the cool scholar casually bringing her baby to a meeting. I should have just brought the stroller.

When the baby and I walked in, several other students were already sitting at the table in the center, beginning to spread out laptops and printed drafts. The faculty member supervising this meeting was the scariest one, someone I'd loved as a professor for his hard questions in class and feared in my exams for the same reason.

As soon as I started speaking about my draft, what I was trying to do and where I was feeling stuck, the baby began grumbling and fussing in his car seat. I waggled an octopus toy above his head half-heartedly, then when he was still unhappy, I unbuckled him and picked him up. The other members of the club began offering their ideas and advice—articles I might read, places where my evidence seemed strong, suggestions for how to clarify my argument—and I held a pen in one hand, trying to record their ideas in my notebook, while with the other hand I held the baby and bounced him on my lap a little. He stood on my legs and reached first for my earrings, then my ponytail. He grumbled and fussed.

After a moment, the faculty member reached his arms out, gesturing that he would take the baby. I'd forgotten: he was a scholar and a rhetorician, but he was also a dad. His wife was a doula and a midwife. As the other students spoke and

I scrambled to write down their ideas, he bounced the baby. The baby, of course, didn't know anything about my professor's professional standing and was happily plucking the pearlized buttons on his Oxford shirt and grabbing at his chin. When we reached the end of the discussion of my chapter and I looked over at them, the professor had bent down to surreptitiously sniff the top of the baby's head. I wondered how long it had been since he'd held a baby and what he was remembering when Penn reached out to grab the collar of his shirt.

I couldn't actually be two people at once, or at least I couldn't do it by myself. I couldn't simultaneously comfort my baby and improve my scholarship. But I could manage them both with help. With a community of writers and thinkers and friends around me, I could.

Creating the Village

It's perhaps obvious that Mead, no matter how much she loved her daughter, was never going to be a happy housewife. Instead, she created what she called a "composite" household. For most of Catherine's childhood, they had a kind of communal household with the sociologist Larry Frank and his large family, which included the five children from his first marriage; Mary, the young Irishwoman he'd married after his first wife's death; and their new baby. During the school year, the families shared a five-story brownstone in Greenwich Village, and in the summer, they went to the Franks' home in New Hampshire. Catherine remembers the situation being described as a "utopia." Mead crafted this communal household not only because it allowed her to continue working, but because it was what she thought was best for children. Catherine would remember later that her mother believed it was "not only possible but preferable that children feel a part of several households and have several caretakers." Catherine wrote that she "did not grow up in a nuclear family or as an only child, but as a member of a flexible and welcoming extended family."

Mead didn't go back into the field for many years after Catherine's birth, but she did travel frequently to speak. And when the United States entered World War II, Mead moved to Washington to work alongside Ruth Benedict on the Committee for Food Habits, a unit of the National Research Council, where Mead planned to practice "applied anthropology." At first, Bateson stayed in New York with Catherine and the Frank family and a nanny, while Mead lived in Washington with Benedict, traveling home as often as she could to visit her family. Even after Mead and Bateson divorced and Bateson moved to California, Mead continued traveling frequently for work, sometimes for long stretches. The rule she made for herself, her daughter remembered later, was that she would always leave Catherine either with a familiar person or in a familiar place, believing that one element of stability would be enough.

What a marvel: Mead created the village we're told it takes to raise a child. And it sounds, in many ways, like a dream of a childhood: the school year in New York, then summers in New Hampshire, a whole pack of children to play with and a group of adults who actually enjoyed each other's company. In New Hampshire, Mary and Bateson danced; the whole extended family put on plays, with elaborate costumes and rehearsals spanning weeks; Bateson got his driving license and drove the Franks' Model A around the property. Catherine says she remembers those summers as "a place where there was no anger and no grief, where each child was cared for by enough adults so that there need be no jealousy, where the garden bloomed and the evenings ended in song."

Mead was frequently gone in Catherine's childhood, and even when she was in New York, she shared the care with other adults. But she was deeply involved in her daughter's life. Catherine remarked that it was only later, when she became a working mother herself, that she understood what she called "the complex infrastructure of my mother's life, the number of people involved in looking after me in the afternoons, getting me home, coming over to cook dinner, and of the way in which my life has been enriched by the diversity of these arrangements and the different kinds of people with whom my life was linked."

This was not the cold, nanny-raised childhood that seems to have spurred so much of Bowlby's work and his insistence that mothers be constantly available for their children. Instead, Catherine remembers both of her parents as deeply present when they were with her, even if they were not with her all the time. "Margaret and Gregory both spent long hours with me," she wrote, "hours when I felt that for the moment at least each was fully mine with no other competing concern." Better an hour's attention than a whole week's worth of distracted care-giving, Mead might have said. And that deep attention comes to feel like our most powerful form of love.

• • •

This is not to say that her mother's absence didn't matter. Even as an adult, Catherine remembered clearly that no matter how well she was cared for in her parents' absence, she still longed for them. "There were all these beloved people," she wrote about the adults and children who surrounded her throughout her child-hood, "yet often the people I wanted most were absent."

But what else could Mead have done? She could have, possibly, left her career behind when Catherine was born, the way Harlow's first wife, Clara, left graduate school when she married him. She could, like Ursula Bowlby, have worked away at a book for more than a decade while raising children and taking a back seat to her husband.

What's remarkable about Mead is that she just refused to choose. She'd have a child and a career, a husband and lovers, a home with friends in New York and long speaking and research trips abroad. Mead's adventurous life served as an example for her daughter, who decided, after a summer trip with her mother to Israel, to stay on and finish high school there on her own. That year in Israel, where Catherine studied Hebrew and began learning Arabic, sparked her interest in languages, inspiring her academic career in linguistics and the many years she'd spend living abroad, including in Iran during the revolution.

And Mead's parenting, and her research more broadly, was animated by much bigger questions than those that obsessed Bowlby and Ainsworth. While attachment theory proponents studied maternal deprivation and made charts showing how long a baby had been held, Mead was asking a bigger question: in Catherine's words, "'What kind of world can we build for our children?'" Mead was working to build that world through her work, as well as in her daughter's life. But the way she built that world wasn't, as Bowlby would have urged, by giving up her "fiddly little" job so she could be constantly by her daughter's side. Rather, Mead enmeshed Catherine and herself within a network of families, and she worked on behalf of that whole community, not just the child living in her own home. She was deeply involved in the progressive elementary school she'd chosen for Catherine. As Catherine remembered it later, "She set out to create a community for me to grow up in, she threw herself wholeheartedly into the planning and governance of my elementary school, and she built and sustained a network of relationships around herself, at once the shelter in which I rested and the matrix of her work and thought." For Mead, a mother wasn't someone who stayed home with her child, but someone who brought her child into a community and worked to make that community stronger for every family.

Mead's life, as described by her daughter, suggests something I find incredibly hopeful: that one way to be a mother is by really knowing your child, and allowing yourself to be really known by them. I think of this when my sons come into my office at home and see the pieces of a book taped up on the wall or scattered across the bed, or when I make them wait for help until I've finished a sentence. Though I've read countless interviews with writers who say that the hard thing about being a mother and a writer is that you can't shut the door against your children, I do shut my door sometimes. And I also invite them in so that my sons will know me as a writer and a thinker, not just their mom. So much of our present-day parenting culture insists that once you've become a mother, that's the most important thing about you. But even after her daughter's birth, Mead remained herself: loving, joyful, good at gathering a whole community, but also doggedly ambitious, obsessed with her work. Mead never tried to make herself into a *good mother*, by the standards of her day, or ours. She brought her whole self to her child.

Or most of it. The moment in Catherine's book when she seems most hurt by her mother is not in describing her frequent absences, but when she receives a letter her mother wrote to be shared only after her death. In this letter, written first in 1955 with the instructions to be given to a select list of people only

upon her death, Mead alluded to the romantic and sexual relationships she'd had with women throughout her life and the
need she'd felt to keep those secret. Catherine seems pained by
this—not the revelation of her mother's sexuality, but the fact
that she'd kept this part of herself hidden. This hurt—that she's
surprised by an element of her mother's life and has to, after
her mother's death, learn something new again without being
able to talk to her about it—seems like further evidence of how
well she'd felt she knew her mother. To have to re-see everything
about your mother's life, and by extension your own, but to do
it only after her death, when she wasn't there to answer. It must
have felt like grieving twice.

My Own Warm, Friendly People

Like Mead, I'd wanted a child—desperately and suddenly, with
a full-body longing that startled me with both the speed of its
arrival and its insistence—and I also needed time and space to
be a person apart from him. And once I had that space, ensured
by daycare, baby dates with friends, a more reliable nap schedule
and better sleep at night, I was more able to delight in being with
the baby. I was more able to fully see him as a person and see the
world he was beginning to explore.

Also like Mead, I enlisted the help of many warm, friendly
people to help us in that first year. In Penn's first weeks, I'd
wanted to hide inside until I figured it out, until I could show
the world what a good mother I was, but in time I learned to let
myself be seen. The "baby dates," as we'd come to call our weekly
meetings, continued that spring. On Tuesday afternoons, Penn
and I met Ana and Lauren at a coffee shop, and on Thursdays
we went to swim lessons at the Y. I was still swamped sometimes

by competing demands—grading and writing and childcare—but I wasn't alone.

We're so often told that we need "mom friends," but the pace and structures of American life make it so that for most of us, our "village" is reduced to a group text or emojis tapped out in the comments of Instagram posts. The kind of ongoing shared care that Mead believed was best for children is really difficult when you have long work hours, a tiring commute, evenings packed full of extracurriculars. Mead's own composite household in New York is now wildly beyond the reach of anyone but the super-rich, or perhaps an ordinary family who just happens to have friends with a spare room inside their West Village brownstone.

In Madison, the community we had was made possible through material circumstances as well as love. Madison is a small city. Lauren lived *all the way* on the west side, near the zoo where Harlow began his primate research, and she could still make it to our house on the east side in less than twenty minutes. If we met at Chocolaterian, a bakery and coffee shop in the Atwood neighborhood between us, we could split the difference and each be there in less than ten minutes. And there was time, too. Those regular meetings were made possible by the way our time was organized. As grad students, Ana and I both had the kind of flexibility that is both a blessing and a curse. Aside from our teaching and office hours, our time was largely ours to do with as we wanted. Though this could mean work often leaked into evenings and weekends, with no real time away, it also meant that Ana could be available on Tuesday afternoons if she wanted. And Lauren, working at a bakery in town, had the clarity of shift work: when she was not working, she was *not working*. There was no way to take her work home, so those nonwork hours were truly hers. That combination of proximity and unscheduled time is a real rarity in American family life.

. . .

One evening another friend was hosting a wine tasting at the coffee shop near the Capitol Square where she worked. Smith was out of town for work, but I wanted so much to go, to be out in the world with friends, and the baby was just so good and so delightful, I felt certain we could handle it. That evening, sipping tiny samples of wine *and* caring for my baby, I felt confident and chic, finally performing the kind of effortless version of motherhood I'd aspired to. I sat at the little wire table while our friend described the next bottle she'd be opening, the baby on my lap and friends surrounding us. I glanced around the coffee shop, thinking smugly about how confident and carefree I looked.

Suddenly, the baby locked eyes with me and pursed his lips with an unmistakable expression and concentration that could only mean a very full diaper. I scurried with him to the bathroom, transformed instantly from hip mom to very regular mom scrubbing poop off the changing table in the bathroom and also somehow off the walls and ceiling. There was a backup outfit for the baby in the diaper bag, but I wasn't in the habit of carrying a change of clothes for myself, and my pants were soaked on the leg where the diaper leaked through. I scrubbed as best as I could, tearing through an entire pack of wipes before running my own hands under the hottest water possible. When I emerged, the baby clean but my own pants soggy, a friend offered to help us to the car. He took Penn in the car seat while I schlepped the diaper bag of horrors. I'd failed in my performance, but I'd finally learned that accepting help was better than looking like a good mom. I didn't need, as I had in my son's first months, to hide inside with the baby until I could show everyone I was doing it right. I could head out into the world and sometimes be a total mess and trust that that was good enough.

. . .

As unconventional as Mead was in her private life, her public face, especially as she aged, hewed quite a bit more traditional. From 1962–1978, Mead wrote a column for *Redbook* that ranged from brief question-and-answer formats to longer essays, covering topics from sex and marriage to bisexuality and working mothers. And while her advice was generally in line with the norms of the time, it's surprising to hear the woman who'd earned a PhD and raised her own daughter in a communal household advise readers in her first column, in January 1962, that college education for women was a "kind of disaster insurance," necessary only as a safeguard if they did not marry or if their marriage ended in divorce. It was ideas like these that led Betty Friedan to devote an entire chapter of *The Feminine Mystique* to arguing that Mead's focus on women's role as mothers doomed them to that narrow fate.

Mead's advice evolved over her years of writing for *Redbook*, and in October 1970, she wrote a column proposing the idea of a "cluster community" in which a group of families, supported by federally guaranteed annual income, would live side by side. Despite those innovative proposals, during that time, Mead's ideas about gender and the need for women to not become "defeminized" grew more entrenched. It wasn't until the mid-1970s that she decided to support the Equal Rights Amendment, which she had worried was "too antimale."

This disconnect between Mead's own life and the advice she doled out to women in the generations after her is puzzling.

Why was education and a career essential for her, but only an afterthought for other women? Why urge women to commit to marriage, when she had moved so quickly through her own marriages and not been faithful in any of them?

It's unsurprising that Bowlby was dismissive of women's right to work, that Ainsworth used her stature in the field to raise doubts about the effects of daycare on children, that Winnicott claimed credit even for insights that had originally been Clare's, that it took Spock decades to really hear the women who'd been speaking to him, that Harlow treated both his wives as footnotes to his own fame. But I want more from Mead. She lived a revolutionary life, but she kept important facets of that life hidden from the public and her own daughter. If Spock admitted late in his life that his best advice for parents could be found in his work and not his life, the opposite seems true for Mead. She declined to offer her own life as an example to the women who turned to her advice, instead suggesting they take up the narrow roles as wife and mother she'd rejected out of hand.

Mead had been raised among educated women who had high expectations for how she'd use her intellect, but professionally she was often the only woman in the room. I wonder if she imagined herself as special, if she couldn't quite believe the women who wrote to her at *Redbook* had the same potential.

This is the problem of looking for heroes and then looking at them too closely. There is no neat path for any of us to follow. There is still so much work for all of us to do. We are all building the road as we go.

7

Relearning the Nature of Love

I don't know if Harlow ever went back to the zoo where his primate work began, but we did. Penn loved the giraffes and the ostriches, their comically oversized legs and knobbly knees, and he'd watched, riveted, as the lemurs dangled and swung in the tower outside the Primate House where Harlow began his career. The Primate House where Harlow first worked with the orangutans Maggie and Jiggs and the baboon Tommy had been built in 1929, just before Harlow's arrival in Madison, and was renovated in 1995. Though Harlow would likely not have recognized much about the zoo, it still housed orangutans like the ones he'd studied in his first years at Wisconsin. And since Harlow's day, as orangutans have become critically endangered, the Henry Vilas Zoo has begun participating in an orangutan breeding program to bolster the worldwide population.

Penn watched the flamingos, whose feathers acquired their trademark variegated shades of pink, I'd read on a placard beside the display, from the brine shrimp and algae in their diet. I watched the baby taking in the world.

. . .

In late August, driving home after a morning at the Children's Museum, the baby beginning to doze off in his car seat behind us, I floated something I'd been thinking about for weeks: "Now's as good a time as any to talk about another baby, right?" We'd had a basically perfect day. I loved this baby, I loved our life, and I wanted more of it. The way to get *more* seemed, obviously, to have another baby.

I'd known that Smith wouldn't exactly be excited about the idea. I was the one who'd wanted a baby in the first place, and I'd been so difficult in those early months, weeping and raging. But after all, it was my body that I was proposing carry the baby, my sleep that would be disrupted, my nipples made sore by the first weeks of breastfeeding. I had a plan, and there was a logic to it: two babies, two years apart. That was what my older stepsisters had done, what my mother and my aunt had done, what I'd always assumed was right and normal. I'd expected Smith would, as he had when I'd started talking about the first baby two years before, go along with it.

Instead, the air inside the car stilled and eventually, painstaking moments later, as we drove down East Johnson and neared the turn for our street, Smith answered: *I'm not sure.* Those early months with Penn, he told me—how anxious and stressed-out I was—were really hard on him. He didn't know if he could do it again. My brain filled with a buzz like radio static. I had not thought that a future of no more babies was possible.

In that moment, I was certain it was my fault: if I'd been a better mother when our baby was new, if I'd been less of a nightmare as a wife, he wouldn't be saying no now. If I could have just done better, been calmer, worked harder at being relaxed. I know: I can hear it now, that paradox of working harder, aiming ever more intensely at perfection. I couldn't hear it then.

We were silent the rest of the way home. Those months *had* been hard. They were hard for me, as I cried and raged and cried. I felt terrible, and I felt alone. When I was having a bad time, my husband was having his own bad time, too. I hadn't realized how alone he felt, too. How alone we'd both been.

But I was persistent. I tucked the baby in his crib for a nap when we got home, then stood across from Smith in the kitchen, the air between us vibrating with tension. I pressed my palm against the countertop and cried. *You knew this is what I wanted*, I said. Each time the baby outgrew a set of outfits, and he watched me pack them into labeled tubs in the basement, he'd known I was thinking of another baby. He'd watched me, and he hadn't said anything about how he felt.

"You have to be more relaxed," he told me. "I can't do it again like that," he said. I knew what he meant, my dark fury, my frustration, which at any moment could spring open from the locked box of my heart. It wasn't enthusiastic endorsement, but he was agreeing. We'd start trying for another baby.

I'd gotten what I wanted. I didn't push my luck, didn't think to ask about how we might be better partners, might better share the work the second time around. I still understood that labor to be mostly mine. Though I couldn't have articulated it then, I was afraid that if I said I needed more help, I'd lose the chance to have another baby. Because I was the one who'd struggled, I believed I was the one who had to be better.

That afternoon in the kitchen, well rested, standing in the

sunshine with a napping baby upstairs, I was certain I could do it. This was the right time for a second baby. Some of what I felt then was the same visceral longing for a child that had come on me so suddenly two years before. Some of it was practical—I was aiming to go on the job market that fall, and though I'd heard plenty of horror stories about the treatment visibly pregnant people received in academic interviews, I figured that was still preferable to being pregnant in my earliest years on the tenure track. In that moment, the shape of our life was knowable. We lived in a city we loved, had good friends, a great doctor, excellent health insurance. I knew our life after that—as I tried to secure an academic job and tenure, or as I worked on something else, if the job market didn't pan out for me—would be full of unknowns. It made a certain sense to add another baby to the life we already knew, in those wild years when I was flying through a dissertation and trying to start my life as a writer in earnest.

But beneath all that, a secret flickering: I could do it right this time. I'd learned so much—how to swaddle, how to breastfeed, how long it would take until the baby was sleeping through the night. Even though I knew the rules didn't work, that my obsession with finding the right way to do it was in many ways the enemy of love, a part of me still believed that mothering was a skill I was on my way to mastering. This time, I thought, I'd be better. This time I'd be good.

. . .

That fall was my fourth year in the PhD program, and I was geared up to take an early run at the academic job market. The spring before, one of the faculty members in our program had led a meeting about going on the job market and had outlined all the materials we'd need to have prepared when the first set of job ads went up September 1. At least one complete dissertation chapter, he said, and ideally not the introduction. Two job letters, one focused on research and one on teaching. A teaching philosophy. A single-spaced, one-page dissertation abstract. If you couldn't write a substantial page about your dissertation's claims and methods and findings, he warned, you likely hadn't done enough work. I wrote fast all summer and ticked each item off the list. I knew for lots of students coming out of our department, getting a job had been a multi-year endeavor, and I figured I might as well start early, as if the market were a lottery and I was maximizing my entries.

That year, instead of teaching, I was helping run the intermediate writing program, and I was working for the Writing Center, tutoring students and helping faculty across the university with their writing instruction. I was also pregnant again, so nauseous and tired that most afternoons when I returned home from campus I lay flat on the bed until I absolutely had to rise and go get the baby from daycare. I'd gotten pregnant very shortly after that tense afternoon in the kitchen, three single stars across one week in my calendar indicating the days we might have conceived. I'd taken a pregnancy test as soon as it was likely to be accurate, and that morning, when Smith returned from the gym, I'd shared the news. "We're really doing this, aren't we?" he'd said. Not upset, but not excited, either.

On one morning in October, still in the first trimester and trying to tell as few people as possible, I was scheduled to give a presentation on CVs and résumés at the School of Pharmacy on the far west side of campus. I'd worn a loose shift dress and a cardigan, giving myself a little space to conceal my rapidly expanding waist, but the jerky stop-starts of the too-warm bus along University Avenue made the nausea intolerable. I yanked on the yellow cord to signal I wanted to exit and lurched off the bus at a crosswalk. I retched into the bushes along the bike walk, then walked the rest of the way into the shiny new building that housed the School of Pharmacy. I was just two or three minutes late to give a talk to a group of bright-eyed almost-pharmacists, polishing their materials for a job market with prospects much brighter than the ones I was facing.

My dissertation advisor led the meetings to prepare job seekers, and I attended that first meeting early that fall, in the dim seventh-floor conference room. The windows overlooked the lake, but the room was small and the ceiling was low, so the room always felt crowded. I stayed after to nervously share my news. "I'm pregnant again," I said, due in May. He stood across from me and blinked, not responding. "So I'll be visibly pregnant by the time I'm going to MLA and campus visits," I added, to clarify why I was sharing this personal information. If he responded, I don't remember it, which is better than the responses I've heard from other women who got pregnant in grad school.

But why did I feel compelled to share the news at all? Why did I feel I owed this man, whose role it was to support my scholarly work and my career, information about what was happening in my body? I can see now that I'd accepted the suggestion, implicit everywhere, that my body was a liability, and that as his student, my success or failure would reflect on him, too.

• • •

As her own children grew, Peggy, Harlow's second wife, began trying to figure out what was going on with those troubled monkeys raised by the seemingly perfect cloth mothers. Though Harlow and Bowlby had held them up as models of perfect mothers—better than real monkey mothers, Harlow had proclaimed in his "Nature of Love" talk—the babies had grown into disturbed and socially dysfunctional adults, and Harlow's lab was devising methods to treat these monkeys. Peggy and Harry's children, Pamela and Jonathan, were teens by then, and Peggy was working hard to rebuild her career. One former graduate student remarked on how smart Peggy was, and how angry she was about having her own research agenda pushed off to the side by the dual forces of the university's nepotism policy, which had forced her to resign her faculty role when she married Harlow, and the demands of motherhood. "She sat all that time, with all that talent," the student remarked, "on the margins of the university."

Peggy devised an experimental setup she called the "nuclear family apparatus." In the attic of the primate lab, they built a neighborhood of four rhesus macaque families, with mother, father, and babies sharing a cage. The children of the neighborhood could access a shared play space, outfitted with swings, ladders, and ropes, but the entrance was small enough so that the adults could not enter. The children could roam the neighborhood, playing with siblings and peers, dropping by each other's houses, then, when they liked, return home, where mother and father were always waiting. This experiment produced surprising results: though adult male rhesus macaques in the wild are generally not involved in child-rearing and some researchers in the lab had worried they might turn abusive when trapped in the house-cages with their offspring, they tolerated the babies' attention. And the monkeys raised in this unconventional setup did far better than other monkeys raised in the lab, scoring higher on tests of problem-solving and completing those assessments faster.

I admire Peggy for her hard-nosed persistence, her insistence on getting the work right and having her name on the research. The first paper to be published about the apparatus bore only Peggy's name, though she did give credit in a note to the grad student who had designed the play equipment the juvenile monkeys used. Peggy's toughness did not make her friends among the grad students at the lab, who consistently remember her as cold and demanding. She was trying, with those nuclear family studies, to do something bold and new, to learn about systems of relationships beyond just the mother and an infant.

But I also want to step back for a minute and point out what a deeply weird way this is of conducting research. Peggy and the other scientists in the lab were invested in watching monkeys because they had questions about human families. Harlow had long been quick to extrapolate from what he saw among his rhesus macaque mother-infant pairs, whether the mother in question was cloth or monkey, to what was better for human infants and what human mothers could stand to learn from that. His work was cited in a *Redbook* article urging hospitals to allow newborns and mothers to stay together in the maternity ward. When journalists inquired, he was quick to weigh in on child-rearing techniques and, though it's unclear if he participated much in raising any of his own four children, offered up opinions on topics ranging from naps to toilet training. This willingness to leap from monkey to human mothers was a good deal of what made him so popular with the media.

Peggy's nuclear family setup, though it's clever as a research design, bears no resemblance to how rhesus macaque monkeys actually raise their babies. Instead, it's a fantasy of the midcentury American family, one that maybe only ever really existed on television. It's an approach to child-rearing that was only the norm among middle-class white American human families for a historical blip in time, and it's not, as both Mead and Friedan could point out, the best or only way to do it. Peggy didn't put those monkey mothers in pearls and heels, but, honestly, she may as well have. Peggy knew firsthand what it was like to raise children with a man who was rarely home. The monkey fathers in her studies were locked into the experimental design along with their mates and the offspring they'd produced. Those fathers had to stay home and help with their kids. Peggy was a serious scientist and rigorous in her approach to research design, so I imagine she'd hate me saying this, but I can't help but see a bit of wishful thinking in the nuclear family apparatus that kept the monkey fathers at home with their families.

Peggy wanted to learn about families and social networks beyond the mother-infant dyad. But creating a monkey neighborhood is, to put it plainly, a bonkers way to pursue these kinds of questions. There's an easier way to learn the many ways that families work, and Mead and the generations following her in anthropology and sociology and primatology were proving that. But Peggy was hemmed in by her discipline and methods and the materials she had on hand. She had questions about human families, but she had a discipline that demanded experimental rigor and a laboratory protocol, and she had monkeys to use as subjects, so that's the study she designed. Had she been trained into a different discipline, she would have used different methods and asked different questions.

This kind of lab science, whether the subject is a rhesus macaque monkey in the Harlow primate lab or an eighteen-month-old human and his mother in Ainsworth's lab at Johns Hopkins, is remarkably poorly suited to revealing anything about the complexities of human relationships or their interior lives. If we really want to learn about people and what matters to them and how they love and how they know themselves to be loved, we can't do that in a laboratory. As anthropologists have continued to study infancy and childhood in cultures beyond postwar London and midcentury Baltimore, they've found a wide range of parenting practices, but one of the most common themes is shared care. When you look beyond the prescriptive models held up as the ideal in the Strange Situation, you find that there are lots of ways to raise a healthy child.

• • •

After a career spent mostly in support roles, editing articles for Harlow and other researchers in the lab and serving as co-editor, alongside Harlow, for the *Journal of Comparative and Physiological Psychology*, Peggy was finally able to return to a faculty role in 1965, when she was named a lecturer in the Department of Educational Psychology. Just two years later, she was diagnosed with breast cancer. Even as she was grievously ill, she continued working and teaching, determined, when she was finally promoted to full professor in 1970, after nearly twenty-five years at the university, to teach under that title. She died in 1971, at the age of fifty-two. In a memorial piece published in *Child Development*, she is remembered as "a distinguished scientific member of the Society for Research in Child Development," and her dissertation is described as "a classic in the area of children's learning." Her nuclear family research was published only after her death, with one article appearing under her name in 1971, and another, on which she is second author, in 1974.

Peggy was not listed as a faculty member in the psychology department until after her death. Harry was angry about that, and railed, in an interview with *Psychology Today*, that she was added only to make the department's numbers with respect to gender look better. But in that same interview, he continued to defend the nepotism policy that had forced Peggy out of her academic position in the first place, arguing that "being a smart woman she knew it was better to marry a man and lose a job than hold a job and not marry a man." It seems impossible for him to imagine a world in which she wouldn't have had to make that choice, or to consider that maybe marrying him wasn't such a prize. There's so much Peggy might have learned, so many ways her research might have evolved, if she'd had the chance.

Harry was adrift after Peggy's death, his drinking accelerating and his lectures increasingly peppered with bad jokes and sexist remarks. He was still traveling and lecturing widely, and nearly every talk was followed by a wave of letters to the American Psychological Association written by affronted female graduate students. Harry didn't like being alone, and he got back in touch with Clara, his first wife. After their divorce, Clara had married Robert Potter, a kind and gentle man who'd helped raise their sons, and the boys had changed their names from Harlow to Potter to honor their stepfather. Robert Potter died in 1960, and Clara had been briefly married for a third time before divorcing in 1965. When Harry reached out after Peggy's death, Clara was working as a counselor in the school of nursing at the University of Tennessee. The pair remarried in 1972, eight months after Peggy's death. Shortly after this marriage, Harlow retired from the University of Wisconsin after more than four decades in Madison. Harry and Clara moved to Arizona, where Harry took up a position as a research professor, a role that came with a title and an office but no pay. Clara kept a close eye on Harry's drinking and forced him to take up walking to improve his health, though he was beginning to suffer from Parkinson's.

When Harry remarried Clara, he attempted to repair his

relationship with his sons from his first marriage as well. Rick Potter, his younger son, lived in nearby Phoenix, and he and Harry saw each other more frequently after the Harlows' move to Arizona. But Rick was clear-eyed about his parents' role in his life, noting that, despite his father's renewed efforts at this late date, "my mom was the one who loved me and spent time building that bond." Clara had begged him, in their first marriage, to spend time with their sons. He chose the lab instead. This is the lesson about love that Harry knew as well as anyone: you have to be there.

Clara attributed their divorce to her stunted ambitions, and she saw this remarriage as a second chance to pick up the research she'd been forced out of forty years before. She set out to study play, including the kind of play we do by ourselves. Clara was warmer than Peggy, but she lacked Peggy's credentials, and Harry's long-time colleagues and collaborators refused to take her seriously as a scholar. Peggy might have been an "ice bitch," as one of the students in Harry's lab called her, but she was a bitch with a PhD, which Clara lacked. Harry and Clara published an article on play together, and she hoped to work together on a book, at one point proposing the title *The Lands of Love*. Instead, as Harry's Parkinson's progressed, she helped him compile a book of his collected works, *The Human Model*. After his death in 1981, Clara edited another collection of his research. She titled it *From Learning to Love*. She'd never publish the book she'd dreamed of.

The Baby in the World

That spring, when I wasn't traveling or frantically typing the last words of my dissertation, Penn and I went for walks most afternoons after daycare. One sunny Friday, with daycare closed and my work paused, we walked the block from our house to the playground outside the Methodist church down the street. At nearly two, he still had the stiff-ankled gait and outstretched palms of a kid who doesn't quite have all their limbs coordinated. The sidewalks in our leafy neighborhood bumped and rumbled where the roots of huge old oaks and black walnuts had grown through and split the concrete. When we approached a cracked spot in the sidewalk, he reached up for my hand, then dropped it again to rush ahead to the swing set.

I still thought of him as *the baby*, even though he wouldn't be much longer, because his brother was due in about a month. The late-afternoon sun stretched my shadow along the lawn, and I could see the swell of my belly in profile.

When he was brand-new, sleeping long stretches in the day-time and screaming for hours at night, I'd walked these streets with him in endless loops. I'd buckled him into the infant car seat, then dropped the car seat into the stroller so he faced me while we walked. Those walks—my body briefly mine again as I zipped along the sidewalks, the baby nearby and content and for a moment not needing me—were the only times I felt the electric fence that had wrapped my body since his birth begin to loosen.

In those early months, we'd stayed close to home on morning walks, strolling a regular circuit of the blocks behind our house to Eken Park and past the Tip Top Tavern, then home again. I waved at the retirees who sat in folding chairs beneath the shade of their open garage door. In late afternoon, when he began to fuss and the reprieve of bedtime was still hours away, we set off again, walking longer as the days cooled. Some days I walked as far as Tenney Park, where in winter volunteers from the fire department came out with hoses to spray down the pond as it froze so its surface would be smooth for skating lessons and hockey practice. Some days I went farther, through the park and onto the trail along the breakwater that led out into Lake Mendota. From the far end of that breakwater, if I looked closely and squinted and imagined it a bit, I could see where the University of Wisconsin campus touched the shore of the lake. I could very nearly see the brutalist concrete building where I sat for graduate seminars and taught first-year composition, the terrace of the student union where I'd spent hours gabbing after workshops, drinking beers and celebrating birthdays and dissertation defenses. In the earliest weeks of motherhood, that part of my life had felt so far away from me. That stretch of lakefront might as well have been the moon for all I could see myself there. It was impossible to imagine how I'd go back to teaching and writing, when I was so sleep-deprived I could barely sustain a thought from one end of a sentence to the next. That stretch of trail across the water, the *L* it made into the lake, felt thrilling and perilous. I knew we wouldn't teeter over that thin strip of asphalt and into the water, but I could see the catastrophe so clearly. I gripped the stroller handles extra tight until we were firmly back on shore.

Almost two years later, so much was different. Ahead of me, Penn held the chains of the swings, waiting for me to catch up and push him. He cackled as he flew into the air. I tried to teach him how to pump his legs, but when I mimed the motion, he just giggled at me.

We kept walking after he tired of the swing set, and when we reached the crest of the hill behind the playground, Penn paused and pointed to a shape emerging from behind the clouds. *Plane*, I said, looking from the sky to his delighted face. He still didn't have many words, but he loved looking together like this, knowing that he'd seen something and shared it. We stood together in the grass as another plane popped into view. He scooped his fingertips so each hand made a little bowl, then tapped his hands together, using the only one of the baby signs he'd really taken up. *More plane*, he signed, his hands moving faster for emphasis, *More plane*, grinning his huge toothy grin, looking from my face to the sky and back again. Was it a demand—did he think I could fill the sky with planes on his request?—or just a celebration of being here and seeing this thing together? As I watched him watching the sky, his whole small body lit up with delight, I was filled with love unlike anything else I've known.

When he was new and I was cracked open, I couldn't have imagined what it would feel like to love him like this.

In the first hours of his life, I'd looked down at his perfect face in the clear-sided hospital bassinet. The thing I felt most clearly then was not love but amazement. *It's you*, I thought. *You were in there all along*. I'd wanted a baby, but I hadn't known he'd be such a specific person. He'd been swaddled tight by a nurse in labor and delivery, and he stared back up at me out of clear blue eyes.

It wasn't the alchemical experience of instant love I'd been promised by natural parenting types, and it didn't kick off the maternal instincts Bowlby believed in. It was just the start. Harlow was wrong about love, or at least his theories were incomplete. I like best the way that developmental psychologist Alison Gopnik puts it: "We don't care for children because we love them, we love them because we care for them."

Labor Watch

That April, we walked into the Primate House at the zoo mostly because it was a bit cooler than the unshaded walkways outside and had long benches along one wall where I'd be able to sit. At thirty-four weeks into this second pregnancy, I was still mostly feeling good, though the early spring heat and the walking were wearing on me. We parked the stroller outside, near the cylindrical cage where the monkeys sometimes came out to play.

When I sat on one of the benches across from the orangutan enclosure, I noticed a female zookeeper in a zoo polo and khaki pants sitting sideways on a ledge along the plexiglass, holding a clipboard. The enclosure was full of grass and leaves and ropes, a high platform so that the orangutans could climb and swing the way they would in the wild. Inside, an orangutan shifted and sprawled on the ground. The keeper explained she was on "labor watch," meaning that the orangutan was pregnant and due soon. "They don't like it when you look at them directly," she explained, watching her, a fourteen-year-old Bornean orangutan named Kawan, out of the corner of her eye.

I sympathized with that orangutan, as I also felt keenly watched in those months. Later that week, I'd leave for the final conference of the academic year, the last travel I'd be permitted before the baby was born. When I'd asked my doctor about travel in late pregnancy, she warned me that if I went into labor after thirty-six weeks and delivered anywhere other than St. Mary's in Madison, my insurance wouldn't pay for it, so I was very close to being trapped at home by imminent birth and the subsequent baby.

All through that year, at conferences and on campus visits as part of my job search, I'd worn blousy tops and scarves and shapeless dresses that I tricked myself into believing might hide my state. Over lunches and dinners and panel presentations, I silently willed my interviewers to listen to my voice, to pay attention to my brain and not my body. Cautionary tales about the liability of a female body in academia, much less a visibly pregnant one, circulated widely in the online spaces where I went to seek advice and community. ("Best to be a woman in the shape of a robot," commented another writer in a Facebook discussion of the perils of being female in academia. She was noting that being a single woman was sometimes seen as a liability, since some committees assumed that without a partner, she'd be a flight risk, more likely to move around. There really is no right way to be a woman in the workplace.) On those visits, I said nothing about the baby in my belly or the baby at home, not when the student worker at one school walked me around campus and showed me the lovely Quaker daycare and not when male colleagues at dinner talked about bringing their kids to department events, not when, at another school, the women on the committee talked eagerly about the many children of faculty members in the department. It did not seem there was a safe way to engage.

At dinner on one campus visit, the search chair, a single woman with no children, sat beside me. "A glass of wine?" she offered, with something like a wink. I pressed my lips together and shook my head a little, trying to imagine there were any number of reasons I might not drink at dinner beyond the obvious one.

A year later, after not getting that job, I saw her again at a conference. After I said hi, she raised an eyebrow and asked, "How's the baby?" as if to say: *I see you. I knew what you were trying to get away with.*

When I did get a job offer, from the second school I'd visited, I arranged a phone call with the two female search chairs. I took the call on campus, sitting in a chair in the sixth-floor conference room, where two falls before, I'd tucked myself away to talk with the nurse who'd confirmed my first pregnancy and scheduled my prenatal appointment. I looked out over the sailboats beginning to return to the spring lake and asked the questions about teaching loads and service and research support my advisor had suggested. When I asked about salary and if there was room to negotiate, they told me exactly what arguments to use and how many more steps I might get on the pay scale. When I wrote back to the dean and asked for more money, using the arguments they'd suggested, I got it.

At yoga the week before the zoo trip, I'd sat in the room of big-bellied women while we did our check-in. We went around, saying our names, how many weeks we were, and how we were feeling. I was nearing what our instructor, Maureen, had nicknamed the "no-NICU" week, as in, if you made it past thirty-six weeks, you could relax a little because even if your baby was born right then, he'd be big enough to not need to spend time in the NICU. Each time a woman reached that milestone in her pregnancy, we clapped. Everyone shared their ailments, their aches and pains, offered remedies and sympathy for the others.

That week, as I spoke, I surprised myself. "I had such a hard time with my first," I said, my voice catching in my throat. "I'm afraid it will be hard again." I looked down at the growing belly beneath my ribbed maternity tank. My vision went a little soft with the tears that welled up in my eyes. The other women made little sighing sounds. I imagine some understood. But I also imagine some felt as I would have, before I became a mother: *That's too bad for her. I'm glad I won't suffer like that.*

What Makes a Mother

At the zoo in Madison, I stood and watched Kawan, trying to not look at her directly, as the keeper warned, until Penn ran out of patience and grabbed my hand, pulling me away from the exhibit, back to the flamingos, to the zoo train that went through the barn, to the shaded picnic tables where we'd have a snack. On the carousel, he chose the jaguar, and he gripped Smith's hand as they went around and around to the crackly tune of carnival music. Each time the carousel spun around to where I stood, he broke into a bright smile and waved, as if he'd just remembered I existed. I captured the moment with my camera.

· · ·

Orangutans are so closely related to humans that a pregnant orangutan in captivity often gets prenatal care from human obstetricians. While Kawan, the orangutan at the zoo in Madison, was pregnant, the chief sonographer from UW/Meriter Center for Prenatal Care visited every other week to record ultrasound images of the growing baby. They used an old ultrasound machine that the hospital's department of obstetrics and gynecology donated to the zoo when they got new equipment. While human women lay down for an ultrasound, Kawan preferred to remain standing. She also disliked the gel that is typically used on human women, so the doctors used water instead.

For the most part, orangutan delivery is quick, far less painful than in human women. Their pelvises are wider than humans', adapted for life clinging to branches and swinging from trees, and their babies are proportionally smaller, so birth doesn't require the careful set of maneuvers through the birth canal that have to work exactly right in human birth. In the wild, orangutans give birth in their nests, up to one hundred feet in the air. Like human babies, an orangutan infant has large eyes that are open shortly after birth.

· · ·

I mentioned our zoo trip at a prenatal checkup a few weeks later. "I feel like I'm on labor watch, too," I joked, though it wasn't entirely a joke.

My doctor looked up from the measuring tape she was wrapping around my belly to check the baby's size. "Oh, the orangutan had her baby," she answered. "But she's not doing so well. She's not caring for the baby, so the zookeepers had to take over. They wear a vest covered in orange fleece strips so they can teach the baby to hold on tight. I guess orangutans can get postpartum depression, too."

I looked down quickly and blinked hard, hoping the doctor wouldn't see my face. I'd mentioned the orangutan casually and was surprised by the strength of my reaction. Who knew that animals could struggle so much with motherhood? What hope could there be for me, a flawed and angry human woman, if an actual animal couldn't mother her child correctly?

• • •

This kind of maternal failure is strikingly common with orangutans, like Kawan at the zoo in Madison, who've been raised in captivity. She'd been raised by humans and had never seen another mother care for an infant. The first baby Kawan saw was her own.

Baby orangutans are surprisingly small in comparison with their sturdy mothers. At birth, a baby orangutan is typically just over three pounds, small enough to fit in a human palm. An orangutan infant's arms and legs are thin, and their muscles develop later, when they begin climbing trees on their own. The keepers named Kawan's baby Keju, from the Malay word for "cheese," in a clever attempt to draw together her wild origins and her Wisconsin birth.

At first, Kawan attempted to care for the baby. She picked her up, inspected her, cleaned up. But then the baby started screaming, and she put the baby down. After that, she never picked the baby up again. Sometimes she sat beside her and patted her. An orangutan baby who isn't held won't thrive. Clinging to the mother helps the baby regulate its body temperature when it's too small to do that for itself.

The keepers tried to teach Kawan how to mother. They showed her how to comfort the baby when she cried. When they fed the baby with a bottle, they showed Kawan where the baby would nurse. In one video of a baby orangutan being bottle-fed, he lifts his head and wails a little, the way my own babies did when they were tired and fighting sleep.

Orangutan mothering is among the most intensive in the animal kingdom. Orangutans are the world's largest arboreal animals, spending nearly all their time in the trees, and an orangutan baby will cling to their mother through all that treetop travel. For two years, the baby will cling to their mother's chest as she swings through the canopy. At two, the baby will move to their mother's back and stay there almost continuously for another year or two. The orangutan baby will stay close to their mother for at least five years. At three months, an orangutan will begin eating the soft food, mostly fruit, his mother has prepared by grinding it between her teeth. Unlike some nonhuman primates that practice shared care, an orangutan mother is the only one who will hold and feed her baby. An orangutan will nurse her baby for up to eight years, the longest of any primate. They typically nurse until the next baby is born. Because maternal investment is so high, births are spaced eight or ten years apart. A female will have only three or four babies across her lifespan.

The intensity of orangutan mothering—a mother's single-minded devotion to her infant, her jealousy if others in the band come near—feels so much like the approach to motherhood I'd internalized and idealized before becoming a mother. Like those orangutan mothers swinging effortlessly through the trees with their infants clinging to them, I'd imagined I could keep everything I'd loved about my life and just attach a baby to it. Orangutan mothers are the only caregiver their infant needs, and they don't need any help. Except, as Kawan's story illustrates, sometimes they do. When orangutans have been raised in captivity and haven't been able to learn how to mother from watching another orangutan, they struggle. Sometimes they can't learn. Even though animals, whether in the zoo or the lab or the wild, are a deeply imperfect proxy for thinking about humans, when I read about that struggling new orangutan mother, I couldn't help but see myself.

In the first photos of baby Keju that the zoo released, she's clinging to the orange strips of felt on a zookeeper's vest and gazing up at the face above her. Even newborn orangutans have quite strong hands that they can use to cling to their mother. In another photo, the baby orangutan's skinny arm is outstretched, her long, thin fingers reaching up as if in celebration, like a baby high five.

A few weeks after her birth, the keepers introduced Keju to Datu, her father, and he seemed pleased. He made a happy giggling noise and reached his finger out to touch hers. He offered his neck to the baby for her to touch.

. . .

In the final weeks of pregnancy, I reread the newborn sections of the sleep website I'd used with Penn. I washed and rewashed all the newborn onesies, marveling that my toddler had ever been small enough to fit into them, that soon we'd have a new baby who would wear them, too. I folded them and placed them neatly in the little dresser I'd topped with a changing pad in the guest room. I washed the liner for the Pack 'n Play.

And somehow, during all that, I sent my dissertation to my full committee. At thirty-nine weeks, I put on the wedge heels and polka-dot dress I'd worn to my sister's rehearsal dinner two months before, topped it with a white blazer, and walked into my dissertation defense. Before the defense, I sat in my shared grad student office, looking over my notes and trying to figure out which committee member I'd ask to drive me to the hospital if I went into labor before we finished. After an hour or so of conversation, they sent me into the hallway and I waited on a bench in the quiet of the late semester. When I went back in, I was a Dr., and they clapped. A week later, my mom arrived for graduation, and, we hoped, for the baby's birth.

At my department's graduation celebration, I cried through my talk and blamed it on the baby, gesturing at the stomach that was barely visible under my billowing doctoral robes. That day, I was standing in the seventh-floor conference room where so much of my life had happened, where I'd attended meetings and given my first mock seminar papers, where I'd listened to other newly minted PhDs give their talks, where I'd told my advisor I was pregnant again, where I'd practiced the job talk that would help me secure a tenure-track position. Though the old building had long since been torn down, I was also standing in the site that had housed the psychology department in Harlow's day. So that day, as I graduated, with one baby cared for at daycare and the other just about to be born, I was also standing in the same site where Harlow's wives had been unable to achieve their own dreams and get the recognition they deserved. On that very same site alongside Lake Mendota, Peggy was refused full recognition of her labor and her intellect right up until her early death, and Clara was forced out of her graduate studies.

That day, I stood beside my fellow graduates in our doctoral

robes and posed for pictures. Afterward, we stood on the terrace outside Memorial Union. I ate ice cream and chatted with
a faculty member who told me how much she'd loved raising her
sons, how tender they were. My husband and I drove home and
picked up Penn from daycare.

· · ·

The baby was due on a Sunday, two days after graduation. On
Monday morning, there was still no baby, but when I kissed Penn
as he walked out the door with Smith for daycare, in a flash I
knew: that was the last moment he'd be my only baby. With the
dissertation done, graduation over, I was out of projects. I filled
a mixing bowl with warm water and sprinkled Bon Ami cleaner
on the kitchen tiles and scrubbed and scrubbed until the lines of
grout grew bright. Later, my mother said when she saw me clean-
ing like that, she knew the baby was coming soon.

At my doctor's appointment that afternoon, we talked about
induction and scheduled our next appointment for the hospital
in a few days. I didn't want to be induced, but I wanted the baby
to be born, and soon, before my mom had to go back to Pittsburgh, so she could take care of Penn while we were in the hospital and meet the new baby when he was still brand-new. My
doctor said she could strip my membranes, which might help
move things along, if the baby was ready. I lay on the exam table,
my legs spread, and the doctor swiped her gloved fingers through
my vagina, and all at once, a gush of fluid splashed onto the
exam table and the floor. My doctor and I looked at each other,
stunned. My husband spit out, "What? What just happened?"

"That was amniotic fluid," I explained. "She broke my water." Breaking a pregnant woman's amniotic sac like this is a
common form of induction, one that even the natural birth

advocates approve of, but it's supposed to be done in a hospital, not accidentally in your doctor's office at a standard prenatal check.

"What do we do now?" I asked.

"Well, you're going to want to go to the hospital," my doctor said. "You can go home and get your bag, but don't take too long. I'll meet you at the hospital. This baby might come quickly."

By the time we'd gotten our bags and gotten back in the car, I was having contractions, something that had taken hours and hours and lots of Pitocin in my first birth. I writhed in the passenger seat as we drove along Lake Monona toward St. Mary's. Between contractions, I swiped on a bright pink lip crayon.

The baby was born two hours after we arrived at triage, just four hours after the doctor accidentally induced me. He was born so fast that his head was perfect, not compressed and cone-shaped as babies' often are when they've taken longer moving through the birth canal. Our doula Johanna arrived after the birth, and when she knocked on the door, I called out, in the thick of hormonal post-birth bliss, "Come in! We have a baby!" The baby's head was covered in strawberry-blond hair, and I made everyone smell his delicious head. "I'm not getting anything," Johanna said, after lowering her head for a sniff. "I think that's a special new mama thing." She took the first picture of the three of us, my lipstick still bright after that fast birth.

We stayed in the hospital for two days, in the same kind of recovery suite as we had with Penn. We'd had a short list of names before his birth, and once we met him, it seemed clear that Finn was the one that fit. The day after his birth, the nurses arrived to do a checkup and give the baby a shot of vitamin K. The nurses held him on the bed and injected his scrawny newborn chicken leg, and he kicked and howled until I picked him up. When I held him, he stopped crying. "They always know their mothers," a nurse said. My first baby wasn't like that. I know now it wasn't that I was doing anything wrong.

When we went home, Smith held the baby, and Penn sat beside him and wrapped his arms around his little brother. "Nose," he said, pointing at Smith's nose, then his own, then touching a gentle finger on the baby's nose, delighted with this miracle of symmetry. "Nose!"

That first night at home, I laid the baby down to sleep in the Pack 'n Play beside our bed. When he woke, I carried him into the guest room, unwrapped his swaddle, nursed him, and braced myself for the howling that always followed nursing when Penn was a baby. Instead, the new baby sighed and fell back asleep. I held him and stood by the window, looking out into the yard, the darkness barely lit by streetlights. This was what I'd thought motherhood would be, but the difference wasn't me. Each baby was his own person with his own needs. My plans and rules and schedules had never really mattered after all.

• • •

On Friday, when baby Finn was four days old, Penn's daycare was closed for Memorial Day weekend. We'd planned to go to the zoo, but the baby was scheduled for a weight check that morning, so we all went to the doctor's office together first. Penn sat on the exam table and watched as the doctor put Finn on the scale. Suddenly my first baby seemed so huge in comparison. Finn was doing great, the doctor said, and had already gained back four ounces.

At the zoo afterward, I stood outside the Primate House with my new baby held in the blue wrap against my chest. He rustled a little, one tiny wrinkly hand reaching up toward my face. He was content to be wrapped tight against my body. I exhaled.

Another mother looked over and said, "Oh, he's so little! How old is your baby?"

"Just a few days old," I answered. "With that one," I said, pointing to Penn, who was grabbing Smith's hand and pulling him toward the rhinos and the giraffes, "we have to get out of the house!"

. . .

Later that fall, after they coached Kawan for months and tried to teach her how to care for her baby, the keepers finally gave up. It wouldn't be possible to reunite Kawan with baby Keju. In October they sent Keju to Zoo Atlanta to be raised by an experienced mother, Madu. Madu had never birthed any of her own babies, but she'd successfully raised three orangutans before Keju. The keepers called Madu a "super surrogate." They said of Kawan that maybe she just "wasn't ready to be a mom."

When I read about Keju being moved to Atlanta, we were in our new apartment, half a country away in New Jersey, where we'd moved for my new job. With two babies and few friends in the insular shore community, we spent much of that year tired and lonely. The old radiators in the apartment meant that if the kids' room was warm enough, we were freezing, and if our room was warm, the boys were boiling. The kitchen had been reno-vated before we moved in, but cheaply, and a strip of counter-top jutted out with no cabinet below it at a height I was always certain would impale Penn as he tore through the house. But that apartment was also where Penn learned to talk, calling out "Baby brother!" happily when the baby learned to roll over or clutch his own feet or grab a waffle from his brother's plate at breakfast. Finn giggled and grew and learned to walk by chasing his older brother with a walker on the tiled floor.

I wasn't wrong that having two children would be harder. Going anywhere was a tactical operation: snacks and diapers and extra clothes; a baby on one arm, a toddler on the other. But also, some things were easier. When the baby cried or I cried or no one slept, I knew it wouldn't last forever, even if it felt like it at the time. My worry split across my two babies, and dissipated slightly.

In that new place, I wasn't a particular kind of mother. No one had a philosophy or parenting style. Sometimes I put the baby in the Ergo when we walked along the boardwalk, but more often we took the double stroller a colleague at work loaned us, and even in the winter, the boys waved at the ocean together.

We didn't do everything right the second time. Despite my promise to be more relaxed, I still got overwhelmed sometimes, tried to take on too much myself, got mad when the help I hadn't asked for didn't happen. When the baby had a whole winter of ear infections and pink eye and RSV, I was, inevitably, the one to take off work. I was his mother, and I couldn't yet see my way to doing anything else. I learned just enough about invisible labor and mental load to make myself mad, but not enough to figure out how to stop doing so much of it.

The balance started to shift the summer the boys were three and one, when I went away for two weeks to a writing conference I'd applied to on a whim, certain I wouldn't get in. When I was awarded a fellowship, I was panicked at the thought of leaving my babies for so long, but Smith insisted they'd be fine, even though it meant taking care of two toddlers by himself for two weeks straight. They ate popsicles sitting on the kitchen floor each night after dinner. I talked to other writers for hours and left a party early one night to stand in an open field and stare up at the moon, feeling all the space around my body.

It would take years—truly, until the implosion of daily life during the early pandemic—to really shift the caregiving workload, and that happened only because I finally cracked. I was trying to do it all, all the meals, all the management of the kids' online school, all the housework and the worrying, along with my own teaching and writing, and I couldn't do it. If I had been hanging on by a thread before the pandemic, that thread finally snapped in those early weeks when we were all at home. When it became clear that the summer camp I'd meticulously planned months before the pandemic would not run, so there'd be no reprieve from the unbroken weeks of kids at home, I sat on our bed and sobbed. And then my husband got to work. He took over breakfasts and lunches, found a summer camp that was taking appropriate precautions where we enrolled the kids.

What I've realized since then is this: nearly every part of parenting is learned, not innate in women or magically instilled by giving birth. Anything a stretched-thin mom is doing all on her own is something that she's had to learn to do. So her partner can learn it, too. And a man who genuinely can't, or won't, learn to pack a lunch or soothe a stressed-out kid or schedule a doctor's appointment is not a man you need to stay married to. It took me a long time to learn that railing against structural forces in a classroom or sharing snarky Instagram posts aren't a substitute for having a tough conversation about what's happening in your own home.

• • •

In Atlanta, Keju grew and thrived with Madu and the other orangutans. At first, the keepers bottle-fed her through the day and night, like a newborn. They trained Madu, the surrogate mother, to bring baby Keju up to the mesh barrier in the orangutan enclosure so they could bottle-feed Keju without contact. Keju bonded with her surrogate mother quickly and clung to Madu tightly the way an orangutan baby should.

Watching the videos of the pair together, I thought about all the women who've mothered me, who taught me how to mother. I remembered standing outside the Malt House with Penn, two months old and howling, how Lauren took him from me and held him, draped a swaddle over him to block out the sound and light until he was soothed and dropped off to sleep. I remembered the day at book club that another friend, a former nanny, took Penn and walked around her apartment with him, talking to him and showing him how the late-afternoon light filtered through her screen door. I thought of all the women who'd listened to me complain about sleeplessness and breastfeeding, who'd answered my emails and text messages and commented under my photos on Instagram, who'd held the baby so I could eat a muffin or just relax. I'd become a mother not in the delivery room, but across those long hard months when women who loved us both sat beside me. I imagined that if Kawan had had Madu beside her to encourage her, to show her how to hold the baby, to not feel fear when the baby cried, she might have become a better mother. Even in the animal world, giving birth isn't what makes a mother.

In a photograph of the two together at seven months, Madu is suspended upside down, her hands and feet wrapped around a rope. Keju is perched on her surrogate mother's back, with her long arms extending around her neck. The hair that was short and bristly right after birth is now longer, the bright orange red orangutans are famous for. Keju stares at the photographer, her hair flaring out around her like a crown.

But on that day in the zoo, Keju was still inside the Primate House, tucked away from visitors, maybe being bottle-fed or clinging to the orange fleece she'd been given as a kind of security blanket. The keepers trained Keju to cling to the fleece strips, to lie on the ground by herself without crying. I was once again a new mother to a new baby, wearing a nursing bra and a heavy pad to catch the postpartum bleeding. But this baby was sleeping. He was going along with my plans.

I know what I look like, I wanted to say, when that woman asked about my baby. With this new baby, sleeping peacefully in the sunshine, I looked like the good mother I'd meant to be. I looked like one of the peaceful baby-wearing mamas I'd envied and been awed by. But it's always messier than the picture strangers see. I was still the same imperfect mother. And maybe those seemingly perfect mothers were imperfect, anxious and edgy or sad and self-doubting, like me.

We stood in the sunshine a moment longer. The howler monkeys roared from their cages, and my toddler once again yanked on my hand, pulling us toward the train and the exit. The new baby wriggled and sighed inside the wrap, his scraggly fingernails itching a little against my chest. My babies pulled me back into the world. We waved once more at the primates and walked toward home.

Coda

"Love Is Not a Given but a Gift"

Before I had a baby I was good. For a long time, as a new mother, I was certain I was bad. I can see now that goodness was the trap.

I will always wish I had been a different kind of mother when my sons were small: more patient, more present, less angry, less swamped by their demands. There is no way back to all the days I rushed through or wished away. Sometimes, when I look at pictures of those baby faces, I feel a deep ache. I miss that sweet soft skin, the tender baby belly in a onesie, or the squish of a baby fist just learning to grab a foot.

But what I know now is how fleeting this time is, too, how before I know it, I'll look back at these days of packed lunches and soccer practice and after-school snacks and wonder where the time went.

Though it's certainly clear by now that I'm deeply skeptical of the leap from animal research to human mothers, there's one study—of rats, of all things!—that's given me a lot of comfort over the years. In the early fifties, when Seymour Levine, a psychologist with a PhD from NYU, wanted to study how stress in infancy might be linked to psychological disorders in adulthood, he began with rats. He created three experimental conditions: rats who were left in their cages to be cuddled by their mothers, rats who were taken out and given a mild electric shock, and rats who would be handled by the researcher but not shocked. (When he applied for federal funding to support the project, who showed up to assess his work but Harry Harlow. Harlow supported the application, and Levine was awarded eight thousand dollars.)

Levine's findings run counter to the model promoted by Bowlby and the attachment theorists who've followed him, that a childhood spent with a devoted mother is the best foundation for healthy adulthood. Instead, the rats who'd been left alone in the cages with their mothers simply couldn't cope when they reached maturity. Released into an open field test, they crouched and peed and wouldn't move. The rats who'd been handled, even the ones who'd been shocked, did much better. Levine's finding? That a little stress is essential in growing a healthy rat. Levine himself is hesitant to make the leap from rats to humans, but I've thought of those shocked rats on so many mornings when I've lost my cool with my kids on our way out the door to daycare or school. They don't need to be constantly cuddled. They don't need me to be perfect. They can survive the little shocks of my failure. Unlike the researchers, I apologize when I've handled my kids a little too roughly and hurt their feelings.

And that, I know now, is what love really is: the daily work of connecting and falling short and making repairs. Attachment theory, as Bowlby and Ainsworth first articulated it, makes such an appealing promise, that if you're good enough to your kids in childhood, you can wrap them in layers of security that will keep them safe throughout their lives. But even if I'd been the kind of perfect mom I'd dreamed of becoming, the kind Bowlby believed a baby needed, that wouldn't have been the best thing for my kids. Instead of one good mom, my sons have two parents who love them, a web of family and friends and neighbors who listen to them and watch them grow. As the early months of the pandemic, when schools and daycares closed, made clear, even two parents isn't nearly enough to care for children. And the work of anthropologists following in Mead's footsteps has borne that out. Though it takes different forms, shared care is the common feature from the Philippines to Congo to Sweden. Families around the world raise children in strikingly different ways, but in basically none of them does the mother do the work alone.

The science beneath our ideals for mothers is just so bad. The studies are riddled with errors and bias, sloppy sampling and methodological shortcomings. And even knowing that, it's still so hard sometimes to set those bad ideas aside. When I can hear the drumbeats of *should*s coming for me—I should make my kid practice his cello more, I should send out a photo Christmas card, I should be worrying more about fruits and vegetables and screen time—I think of an essay a friend wrote about learning to care for herself through a period of chronic pain. She began to think of her brain in the way you'd train a puppy, and when she'd start to spiral, she'd say, *Drop it. Drop it.* So when I hear those *should*s, all those impossible markers of finally becoming a "good mother," coming for me, I whisper to myself: *Put it down.* We can put those bad ideas down.

And those *should*s—all that reaching to meet the ideals that someone else set for us—those all end up being the opposite of how it feels to really love and care for and know another person.

If love isn't instant or automatic, if giving birth doesn't produce an instant bond that makes the labor of caring for a baby automatic, where does that love come from? The French historian Elisabeth Badinter grappled with this question in her controversial book *Mother Love: Myth and Reality*, an investigation of eighteenth-century France, where urban mothers often sent their infants off to wet nurses in the countryside, resulting in long separations and appallingly high infant mortality. Based on that research, Badinter had argued that maternal love isn't innate or instinctive, but arises when mothers have the luxury of caring for their children and are cared for themselves. "Maternal love is not a given but a gift," she said. And when her children were teased at school because of the book, she told them, "Love is not automatic. We built it together. I choose to love you."

My sons are now at the center of their elementary school years. I can't help but marvel at their growing bodies, as they lie on the couch or lounge in bed. *You used to be so small*, I say, showing them how I used to hold them with their head on my shoulder and their feet above my waist, *And now you're this big*, exaggerating for effect, holding one hand at their head and the other stretched to touch the bottom of their feet. *You're just so big.* I was away teaching at a writing conference recently, and when I got home, I told my older son, *I think you got taller even over the weekend*, as I watched him reach for snacks at the top of our pantry. *Of course I did*, he said, *I'm growing all the time.*

And this, I often think, is what motherhood is, the magical ordinary work of traveling through time together. Sometimes when I look at my older son, I get a flash and he's fifteen, his face serious and handsome as he earnestly explains how something works. And sometimes my younger son is still a baby. At the park, running through the overgrown grass, his cheeks pinking with the effort and the heat, I see him as he was at fifteen months, beginning to run, white-blond hair and baby belly in a onesie. When he sits on the couch, he presses his body right against me, or he flops his legs across my lap. Sometimes he rests his hand on my forearm as he pokes the screen of his tablet or stares riveted at cartoons, as if he just needs to know I'm there. We travel through time like this, each of us holding all our past and future selves inside our cells.

My mother kept beautiful baby books for my sister and me. In mine, there are real photographs developed from canisters of film, a lock of hair, funny things we said recorded verbatim, all my milestones marked with the date. Photos of playdates and birthday parties, all the babies from the playgroup lined up on our old navy couch, even when it's clear we're all just one wobble away from toppling over. A note about the day I leaned over in the back seat when my sister was a baby and whispered, *You're my best friend.*

For Penn's first Christmas, when we drove home to Pittsburgh, I sat on the couch at my mother's, with the baby book laid open across my lap and my own baby tucked in beside me. *Don't you wish you could travel back, just for a minute,* my mother said, pointing at a photograph of me at nine months pregnant or so in corduroy overalls, *and tell her all the wonderful things that will happen.* She leaned over to me and said, *I wish that I could travel back in time and hold you as a baby,* cradling her arms as if she could still feel that tender weight.

The baby books I've kept are thin. My sons' lives are captured mostly digitally, and sometimes we stare together into my phone and watch their lives flow backward on Instagram. In those pictures, a baby sleeps in his crib, wrapped tight inside a star-patterned swaddle; I hold the baby, just days home from the hospital and gaze down adoringly at his face. The pictures they love best surprise me: a photo from my older son's third birthday when the baby stole a bite of cake before we'd even finished singing, the Halloween they insisted on the same Catboy costume. Many of them are moments they remember only because they've seen the photographs so many times.

I think about that now, each time I take a picture at a soccer game or school event or ordinary weekday morning. I'm taking it for myself, to hold on to this moment, but now I know I'm taking it for them, too, for the future versions of my sons who will live beyond me, so they'll know that I was here, that I was paying attention, that I loved them this whole time.

Like my own mother, I wish that I could travel back in time and hold my babies longer. And I wish I could tell that other me, the exhausted thin-skinned new mother, that she's doing great, that everything turns out fine. I'd tell her those babies are boys now, so funny and tender and smart.

And look, here they are: freckles and bruised shins and missing teeth and wild cackles and bedtime hugs. We're traveling through time. The love we've made together carries us.

Acknowledgments

Like mothering, writing a book is possible only in community, and there are so many people to thank for being part of that community.

My agent, Maggie Cooper, who saw the potential inside a very different proposal and helped me discover the right shape for this book. My editor, Brigitte Dale, whose smart comments on everything from structure to historical context to co-parenting have improved this book immensely. Thanks to the entire team at St. Martin's Press, including Laura Clark, Rebecca Lang, Sara Beth Haring, Ginny Perrin, Michelle McMillian, and Danielle Fiorella. A special thanks to copy editor Linda Sawicki. Thanks also to early readers, including Lara Bazelon, Emily Bloom, Minna Dubin, Carrie Mullins, Catherine Newman, and Sara Petersen.

A book like this is built on the meticulous research of other writers, and I'm especially grateful to Deborah Blum, whose *Love at Goon Park* was my first entry to the deeper meaning beneath those monkeys and their cloth mothers, and Marga

Vicedo, whose rigorous scholarship on Bowlby, Harlow, and the science of attachment first helped me begin to unpick the tangle of our bad ideas. Thanks also to the contributors to *The Long Devotion: Poets Writing Motherhood*, whose work has helped me to think about so many experiences of mothering beyond my own, and my partner in that project, Emily Pérez.

Thanks to the editors who gave me space and support to think through ideas related to this book: Rebecca Onion at *Slate*, Jess Zimmerman at *Electric Literature*, Matt Ortile at *Catapult*, and Ashlee Gadd at *Coffee + Crumbs*.

Gratitude to Stockton University's Research and Professional Development Committee for summer funding and a sabbatical that supported this project, and to my colleagues in the First Year Studies and Writing programs, particularly Emari DiGiorgio and Emily Van Duyne, whose ambition as writers, mothers, and activists inspires me.

We were so lucky in Madison to have a community of friends who became family and who've stayed that way across multiple moves. It's impossible to imagine those earliest years of parenthood without Ana Lincoln, Sean Berger, Lauren Reynolds, Chris Reynolds, and Greg Jones. My Madison writing group— Rebecca Dunham, Cynthia Marie Hoffman, Jesse Lee Kercheval, Rita Mae Reese, and Angela Voras-Hills—helped me stay in touch with the creative part of my brain through babies and a PhD. I'm so grateful to the University of Wisconsin–Madison's MFA program and the doctoral program in composition and rhetoric for the training in writing and research that made this book possible. Special thanks to my advisor Morris Young, whose frequent questions about how my creative and scholarly work might be connected nudged me toward seeing how they are, and Christa Olson, whose mentorship and example have been invaluable. Thanks also to Erinn Batykefer, Leigh Elion, Rebecca Hazelton, Elisabeth Miller, the tutors and staff at the Writing Center, and all the other warm, friendly people who made those years in Madison so special.

I'll forever feel grateful to the healthcare providers—Dr. Stephanie Skladzien, the Aspen Team nurses, and our doula, Johanna Hatch—who cared for me through two pregnancies and births. We were able to access high-quality, affordable healthcare because of the TAA, the graduate worker union at the University of Wisconsin–Madison. In New Jersey, being a member of the Stockton Federation of Teachers, our faculty union, has impacted my professional life profoundly. Every worker and parent deserves this kind of support.

As my research and writing life have taught me, even intellectual work happens in material places, and I'm grateful to the communities that sustained me as I wrote. With thanks to the Vermont Studio Center, the Sundress Academy for the Arts, and the Highlights Foundation for space to write; to Caroline and Tony Grant and the Sustainable Arts Foundation and the New Jersey Council on the Arts for encouragement and financial support; to the booksellers at Inkwood and White Whale for serving as vital sites of community in-person and through online events, and for so many good book recommendations for me and my kids; to Murphy Writing and the Getaway, Blue Stoop, the Writers House at Rutgers-Camden, and Inprint for demonstrating, again and again, the magic that happens when writers come together; to Jami Attenberg and the #1000words community for encouragement and accountability; and to the owners and members of Upcycle and Hub868, where so much of this book took shape.

With thanks to our friends and neighbors in New Jersey,

many of whom have heard me talk through the ideas of this book at school pickup or standing on the sidewalk while our kids scribbled in chalk or scooted to the end of the block. Nothing in my professional life or my writing life would be possible without the childcare providers and public school teachers who loved and taught my children through the years it took to write this book, and I'll always be grateful for their skilled care and in awe of their expertise. A note of special appreciation for Kaite Yang and Dan O'Brien, who had plenty of opportunities to witness the chaos of life with small children at our house and were brave enough to have a baby anyway. Your encouragement and interest in this book has meant the world to me.

I'm also grateful for the online writing communities and friendships that supported my writing practice, especially across the pandemic. My writing groups with Diana Dube, Maggie Lowe, and Val Woolley and regular check-ins with Kelly McMasters and Jill Vegas were a vital part of writing this book. Many thanks to Heather Bowlan, my poetry sister and best friend.

I still marvel at my good fortune to have been raised by and among smart, determined women who gave me so many models of how to be a mother: Jeanne Nash, Marilyn Seigh, Ellen Reddy, Martha Nash, Anne Gary, Annie Hartley-Martin, and Megan Haines.

With love to Smith. I'm so proud of what a team we've become.

For my sons. Getting to be your mom is the luckiest thing in my life.

Notes

Introduction: "Love Is a Wondrous State"

4   **"love is a wondrous state":** Harry Harlow, "The Nature of Love," *The American Psychologist* 13, no. 12 (1958): 673.

5   **It sometimes feels like every generation of mothers:** For Friedan and Rich, see Betty Friedan, *The Feminine Mystique: 50th Anniversary Edition* (New York: W. W. Norton & Company, 2013); and Adrienne Rich, *Of Woman Born: Motherhood as Experience and Institution* (New York: W. W. Norton & Company, 1995). For more on family in the postwar era, see Elaine Tyler May, *Homeward Bound: American Families in the Cold War Era* (New York: Basic Books, 2017).

6   **our standards for mothers have always increased:** Andrea O'Reilly, *Mother Outlaws: Theories and Practices of Empowered Mothering* (Toronto: Women's Press, 2004): 10.

7   **It's becoming ever harder to resist:** For more on intensive parenting, see Sharon Hays, *The Cultural Contradictions of Motherhood* (New Haven, CT: Yale University Press, 1999) and Claire Cain Miller, "The Relentlessness of Modern Parenting," *New York Times*, December 25, 2018, https://www.nytimes.com/2018/12/25/upshot/the-relentlessness-of-modern-parenting.html.

7   **"Wherever women have":** Sarah Blaffer Hrdy, *Mothers and Others: The Evolutionary Origins of Mutual Understanding* (Cambridge, MA: Harvard University Press, 2011), 9.

7   **As cases from Ohio to Texas have demonstrated:** When I first wrote this sentence, I was thinking specifically of Brittany Watts, a Black woman in Ohio who was arrested after miscarrying a fetus, and Kate Cox, a white woman in Texas who was refused an abortion in that state, even after doctors determined her

fetus had a fatal diagnosis and that carrying the pregnancy posed grave risks to her health. As I write this note, several months later, there have been more women harmed and traumatized because of laws that deny them compassion and care, and by the time you read this, there will be still more.

9   **"The trick is"**: Tessa Fontaine, "The Trick Is There Is No Trick," *The Rumpus*, July 22, 2013, https://therumpus.net/2013/07/22/the-trick-is-there-is-no-trick/.

1. A Perfect Monkey Mother

16   **Across town, on the University of Wisconsin campus:** Harlow described his early years at Wisconsin and the development of the cloth mother studies in "Birth of the Surrogate Mother," *Discovery Processes in Modern Biology*, ed. W. M. Klemm (Huntington, NY: R. E. Krieger, 1977). Other biographical details come from Deborah Blum, *Love at Goon Park: Harry Harlow and the Science of Affection* (New York: Basic Books, 2002). Details about Bowlby's biography and early research come from Marga Vicedo, *The Nature and Nurture of Love: From Imprinting to Attachment in Cold War America* (Chicago: University of Chicago Press, 2013), and Michal Shapira, *The War Inside: Psychoanalysis, Total War, and the Making of the Democratic Self in Postwar Britain* (Cambridge, MA: Cambridge University Press, 2013).

18   **"The controls are perfect"**: Blum, *Love at Goon Park*, 100.

20   **"These are not just monkey stories"**: Harlow, "Birth of the Surrogate Mother," 140.

21   **In the early 1950s:** Harlow, "Birth of the Surrogate Mother," 146.

22   **"born in a Boeing stratocruiser"**: Harlow, "Birth of the Surrogate Mother," 146.

22   **"soft, warm, and tender"**: Harry Harlow, "The Nature of Love," *The American Psychologist* 13, no. 12 (1958): 676.

23   **"brightened with sudden insight"**: Harlow, "The Nature of Love," 676.

24   **"mother-love is a dangerous instrument"**: John B. Watson, *Psychological Care of Infant and Child* (New York: W. W. Norton & Co, 1928): 81–82.

24   **"perhaps all you've known"**: Blum, *Love at Goon Park*, 2.

24   **earlier psychologists:** This idea of love as merely a conditioned response to stimulus has its roots in both the behaviorist psychology of Watson and the Freudian belief that a child's first relationship is not with his mother but with her breast. Harlow asserts that this idea that an infant's love is merely a response to being fed was a "position commonly held by psychologists and sociologists" in his 1958 talk "The Nature of Love," and John Bowlby presents the idea of cupboard love as one theory to be refuted in his article "The Nature of the Child's Tie to His Mother," published that same year. Blum discusses this history in *Love at Goon Park*, 56–57.

25   **in a photograph:** Harlow, "Love in Infant Monkeys," *Scientific American* 200, no. 6 (June 1959): 69.

25   **Bowlby's work:** Bowlby spent decades articulating and elaborating this theory and defending it from criticism; the earliest explanations of it can be found in

his 1951 WHO Report and the 1958 "The Nature of the Child's Tie to His Mother."

26   **As a small child:** Bowlby's son Richard Bowlby recounted this episode from his father's childhood when he gave the Donald Winnicott Memorial Lecture in 2004. The younger Bowlby commented that, as his father was working on the research that would become *Forty-Four Juvenile Thieves*, "I imagine my father identified the loss of his Minnie with the maternal deprivation experienced by the delinquent children in the school." Sir Richard Bowlby, *Fifty Years of Attachment Theory : The Donald Winnicott Memorial Lecture* (Oxford: Taylor & Francis Group, 2004): 13.

27   **"a rather one-track":** J. M. Tanner and Barbara Inhelder, *Discussions on Child Development* (New York: International Universities Press, 1971), 27.

27   **an estimated thirteen million orphans:** Estimates on the number of children orphaned by the war vary widely; my number comes from Frank C. P. van der Horst et al., "A Tale of Four Countries: How Bowlby Used His Trip Through Europe to Write the WHO Report and Spread His Ideas," *Journal of the History of the Behavioral Sciences* 56, no. 3 (Summer 2020): 170, doi:10.1002/jhbs.22016.

27   **His report on the matter:** John Bowlby, "Maternal Care and Mental Health," *Bulletin of the World Health Organization* 3 (1951): 355–534.

28   **"What Makes a Child Grow Up":** Shapira, *The War Inside*, 230.

28   **Bowlby's report was reprinted:** Inge Bretherton, "The Origins of Attachment Theory: John Bowlby and Mary Ainsworth," *Developmental Psychology* 28, no. 5 (1992): 761.

28   **"a warm, intimate, and continuous relationship":** Bowlby, "Maternal Care and Mental Health," 73.

29   **more than one and a half million mothers:** Nancy Cott, *Public Vows: A History of Marriage and the Nation* (Cambridge, MA: Harvard University Press, 2000): 191.

29   **a 1955 *Life* magazine article:** "An Adopted Mother Goose: Filling a Parent's Role, a Scientist Studies Goslings' Behavior," *Life Magazine* 39 (July/August 1955): 73–74, 77–78.

29   **he'd been a member of the Nazi party:** Vicedo, *The Nature and Nurture of Love*, 48–49.

30   **"closely akin to a research program":** Frank C. P. van der Horst, Helen A. LeRoy, and René van der Veer, "'When Strangers Meet': John Bowlby and Harry Harlow on Attachment Behavior," *Integrative Psychological and Behavioral Science* 42 (2008): 370–388.

32   **"lactation is a variable":** Harlow, "The Nature of Love," 676–677.

32   **the brains of gay dads:** Chelsea Conaboy, *Mother Brain: How Neuroscience Is Rewriting the Story of Parenthood* (New York: Henry Holt and Company, 2022).

32   **"anyone can be a mother":** Vicedo, *The Nature and Nurture of Love*, 159.

37   **"the future of a child's mind":** Marga Vicedo, "The Social Nature of the Mother's Tie to Her Child: John Bowlby's Theory of Attachment in Post-War America," *The British Journal for the History of Science* 44, no. 3 (2011): 401.

2. Overly Attached

40   **"Just as the baby needs"**: John Bowlby, "Maternal Care and Mental Health," *Bulletin of the World Health Organization* 3 (1951): 355–534.

41   **"the danger of racketing about"**: Frank C. P. van der Horst et al., "A Tale of Four Countries: How Bowlby Used His Trip Through Europe to Write the WHO Report and Spread His Ideas," *Journal of the History of the Behavioral Sciences* 56, no. 3 (Summer 2020): 173, doi:10.1002/jhbs.22016.

41   **"to gather evidence"**: van der Horst et al, "A Tale of Four Countries," 171.

41   **monotropy**: John Bowlby, "The Nature of the Child's Tie to His Mother," *International Journal of Psycho-Analysis* 39 (1958): 350–373.

41   **"very doubtful"**: van der Horst et al, "A Tale of Four Countries," 173.

44   **recorded her own experience**: Lynda R. Ross, "Reading Ursula Bowlby's Letters (1939–1940): A Chronicle of First-Time Motherhood," *Journal of the Motherhood Initiative* 5, no. 1 (2014): 67–82, https://jarm.journals.yorku.ca/index.php/jarm/article/view/39341.

45   **"wouldn't send a dog away"**: Joseph Schwartz, *Cassandra's Daughter: A History of Psychoanalysis* (New York: Viking Books), 225.

45   **Ursula wrote in her journals**: Ross, "Reading Ursula Bowlby's Letters (1939–1940)," 78.

49   **"When I began making A's"**: Deborah Blum, *Love at Goon Park: Harry Harlow and the Science of Affection* (New York: Basic Books, 2002), 66.

50   **"ice bitch"**: Blum, *Love at Goon Park*, 129.

50   **Harlow allowed that a woman *might***: Blum, *Love at Goon Park*, 235.

51   **his longtime secretary Helen LeRoy**: Helen A. LeRoy, "Harry Harlow: From the Other Side of the Desk," *Integrative Psychological and Behavioral Science* 42 (2008): 350.

51   **"My father had had children"**: Blum, *Love at Goon Park*, 132.

52   **"remains widespread"**: Natalie Kitroeffer and Jessica Silver-Greenberg, "Pregnancy Discrimination Is Rampant Inside America's Biggest Companies," *New York Times*, February 8, 2019, https://www.nytimes.com/interactive/2018/06/15/business/pregnancy-discrimination.html.

52   **The gender wage gap is**: Kitroeffer and Silver-Greenberg, "Pregnancy Discrimination Is Rampant."

53   **This parenthood pay gap persists**: Claire Cain Miller, "Children Hurt Women's Earnings, but Not Men's (Even in Scandinavia)," *New York Times*, February 5, 2018, https://www.nytimes.com/2018/02/05/upshot/even-in-family-friendly-scandinavia-mothers-are-paid-less.html.

53   **"I do not agree"**: Blum, *Love at Goon Park*, 91.

53   **"the second wave of feminism"**: Lucy Cooke, *Bitch: On the Female of the Species* (New York: Basic Books, 2022), xviii.

54   **"The males of almost all animals"**: Charles Darwin, *The Descent of Man, and Selection in Relation to Sex* (John Murray, 2nd ed., 1879; republished by Penguin Classics, 2004), 256–257.

54   "'the home economics' of animal behavior": Sarah Blaffer Hrdy, *Mothers and Others: The Evolutionary Origins of Mutual Understanding* (Cambridge, MA: Harvard University Press, 2011), 46.

54   comparative psychologists studying maternal behavior: Hrdy, *Mother Nature*, 28–29.

55   Harlow described: Harry Harlow, "The Monkey as a Psychological Subject," *Integrative Psychological and Behavioral Science* 42 (2008): 336–347, https://doi.org/10.1007/s12124-008-9058-7.

55   "a constant trend among psychologists": Harlow, "The Monkey as a Psychological Subject," 341.

56   "a central nervous system": Harlow, "The Monkey as a Psychological Subject," 343.

56   "but they seldom become": Harlow, "The Monkey as a Psychological Subject," 346.

56   "often marveled at the sight": Harlow, "The Monkey as a Psychological Subject," 343.

56   One scientist, Jeanne Altmann: For more about Jeanne Altmann and how her work revolutionized the field, see Jeanne Altmann, *Baboon Mothers and Infants* (Chicago: University of Chicago Press, 1980). Hrdy's *Mother Nature* and Cooke's *Bitch* both have excellent discussions of Altmann's work and its significance both for understanding primate mothering and for its groundbreaking research methods. The 1974 paper that articulated her methodology, "Observational Study of Behavior: Sampling Methods," has been cited nearly twenty thousand times.

60   one biographer referred to her: Brett Kahr, "Ursula Longstaff Bowlby (1916–2000): The Creative Inspiration Behind the Secure Base," *Attachment: New Directions in Psychotherapy and Relational Psychoanalysis* 10 (December 2016): 223–242.

3. An Ordinary Devoted Mother

66   he began by assuring women: Donald W. Winnicott, "Getting to Know Your Baby," in *The Collected Works of D. W. Winnicott: Volume 2, 1939–1945*, ed. Lesley Caldwell and Helen Taylor Robinson (Oxford: Oxford University Press, 2016): 221–226.

66   nearly 50 percent: Michal Shapira, *The War Inside: Psychoanalysis, Total War, and the Making of the Democratic Self in Postwar Britain* (Cambridge, MA: Cambridge University Press, 2013), 116.

67   "it has been the only English book": Brett Kahr, "Ursula Longstaff Bowlby (1916–2000): The Creative Inspiration Behind the Secure Base," *Attachment: New Directions in Psychotherapy and Relational Psychoanalysis* 10 (December 2016), 225.

67   "a renowned public figure": Anne Karpf, "Constructing and Addressing the 'Ordinary Devoted Mother,'" *History Workshop Journal* no. 78 (Autumn 2014): 101.

67   Nearly eight million British women: Shapira, *The War Inside*, 59.

68 **"the glass and rubble":** Brett Kahr, *D. W. Winnicott: A Biographical Portrait* (Oxfordshire: Taylor and Francis, 2018), 96.

68 **"So many of my friends":** Judith Issroff, "Introduction," in *Donald Winnicott and John Bowlby: Personal and Professional Perspectives*, ed. Judith Issroff (London: Routledge, Taylor & Francis Group, 2005), 7.

68 **"I hardly noticed the blitz":** Donald W. Winnicott, "Primitive Emotional Development," *International Journal of Psycho-Analysis* 26 (1945): 137.

69 **"I want to be in the hurly burly":** Joel S. Kanter, "Let's Never Ask Him What To Do: Clare Britton's Transformative Impact on Donald Winnicott," *American Imago* 61, no. 4 (Winter 2004): 461.

69 **"a difficult doctor":** Kanter, "Let's Never Ask Him," 461–462.

70 **"Psychoanalysis was not only high theory":** Shapira, *The War Inside*, 5.

71 **His biographer blamed the women:** Karpf, "Constructing and Addressing the 'Ordinary Devoted Mother,'" 95.

71 **writing in to the BBC:** Karpf, "Constructing and Addressing the 'Ordinary Devoted Mother,'" 91.

72 **"No book's rules":** Shapira, *The War Inside*, 131.

76 **"mothers who have it in them":** Donald Winnicott, "The Theory of the Parent-Infant Relationship," *The International Journal of Psychoanalysis* 41 (1960): 592.

78 **"a silent health crisis":** "Mind the Gap," *Postpartum Support International*, accessed March 13, 2024, https://www.postpartum.net/mind-the-gap/.

80 **"terrible interference":** Donald W. Winnicott, "Getting to Know Your Baby," in *The Collected Works of D. W. Winnicott: Volume 2, 1939–1945*, ed. Lesley Caldwell and Helen Taylor Robinson (Oxford: Oxford University Press, 2016), 221.

81 **"extraordinary condition":** Donald W. Winnicott, *The Family and Individual Development* (London: Tavistock Publications, 1965), 15.

81 **"at one extreme":** Winnicott, *The Family and Individual Development*, 15.

84 **One source:** Brett Kahr, "The First Mrs. Winnicott and the Second Mrs. Winnicott: Does Psychoanalysis Facilitate Healthy Marital Choice?," *Couple and Family Psychoanalysis* 9, no. 2 (2019): 112.

84 **Despite the long affair:** Kahr, "The First Mrs. Winnicott," 117–118.

85 **Winnicott's biographers note:** Kahr, *D. W. Winnicott: A Biographical Portrait*, 127.

85 **"fearful" understanding:** Kahr, "The First Mrs. Winnicott," 113.

86 **he once wrote to Arthur Miller:** Kanter, "Let's Never Ask Him," 475.

87 **Twice in the years:** Stuart Roberts, "The Rising Tide: Women at Cambridge," accessed December 17, 2023, https://www.cam.ac.uk/stories/the-rising-tide.

87 **the women who attended Cambridge were ambitious:** Jill Lamberton, "'A Revelation and a Delight': Nineteenth-Century Cambridge Women, Academic Collaboration, and the Cultural Work of Extracurricular Writing," *College Composition and Communication* 65, no. 4 (June 2014): 568.

88 **"quite a considerable achievement":** Kahr, "The First Mrs. Winnicott," 109.

88 **From the beginning of their marriage:** Kahr, "The First Mrs. Winnicott," 109.

88 **Alice was working in the war effort:** Julie Greer, "Alice Buxton Winnicott: The

Paintings of a Pioneering Potter," Art UK (website), May 15, 2015, https://artuk
.org/discover/stories/alice-buxton-winnicott-the-paintings-of-a-pioneering
-potter.

88   **"not because of bombs":** Donald Winnicott, "Hate in the Counter-Transference,"
International Journal of Psychoanalysis 30 (1949): 69–74.

89   **One biographer suggests:** Kahr, "The First Mrs. Winnicott," 105.

92   **"the great absentees":** Vicedo, "The Social Nature of the Mother's Tie to Her
Child," 423.

4. Strange Situation

98   **If the science just reaffirms sitcom clichés:** With thanks to Danielle Carr for
her incisive analysis of the role of attachment styles in pop psychology, in her
January 2022 *Gawker* article, "Don't Be So Attached to Attachment Theory."

98   **Bowlby's older son:** Judith Issroff, "Introduction," in *Donald Winnicott and John
Bowlby: Personal and Professional Perspectives*, ed. Judith Issroff (London: Routledge, Taylor & Francis Group, 2005), 16.

99   **attachment theorists have paid little attention:** Everett Waters and Theodore
P. Beauchaine, "Are There Really Patterns of Attachment? Comment on Fraley
and Spieker (2003)," *Developmental Psychology* 39, no. 3 (2003): 417.

100 **"a Rosetta stone of sorts":** Robert Karen, "Becoming Attached," *The Atlantic*, February 1990, https://www.theatlantic.com/magazine/archive/1990/02/becoming
-attached/308966/.

101 **"attachment-driven interventions":** Paul Michael Garrett, "Bowlby, Attachment, and the Potency of a 'Received Idea,'" *British Journal of Social Work* 53, no.
1 (January 2023): 101, https://doi.org/10.1093/bjsw/bcac091.

101 **"the only thing your child needs":** Karen, "Becoming Attached."

102 **"Attachment-theory proponents tend to see":** Karen, "Becoming Attached," 3.

103 **a study done by two Penn State researchers:** Jay Belsky and Michael J. Rovine,
"Nonmaternal Care in the First Year of Life and the Security of Parent-Infant
Attachment," *Child Development* 59, no. 1 (1988): 157–167.

105 **"a brilliant synthesizer":** Karen, "Becoming Attached"; and Garrett, "Bowlby,
Attachment, and the Potency of a 'Received Idea,'" 110.

105 **Bowlby faced increasing criticism:** This analysis of Bowlby's career and his
reliance on animal research was informed by Marga Vicedo's *The Nature and
Nurture of Love: From Imprinting to Attachment in Cold War America* (Chicago:
University of Chicago Press, 2013).

106 **"supportive femininity":** Karen, "Becoming Attached."

107 **"That plan worked perfectly":** David Maurer, "Never Miss an Opportunity to
Hold a Baby," *Daily Progress*, May 12, 1998.

107 **she was determined to stay in Toronto:** Mary Ainsworth, "Mary D. Salter
Ainsworth: An Autobiographical Sketch," *Attachment & Human Development* 15, no. 506 (2013): 448–459, https://doi.org/10.1080/14616734.2013
.852411.

107 **"the reverse of sex discrimination"**: Ainsworth, "An Autobiographical Sketch," 452.

108 **"uncomfortable" for Len**: Ainsworth, "An Autobiographical Sketch," 453.

109 **"an anthropological component"**: Ainsworth, "An Autobiographical Sketch," 455.

110 **"despite all the language and other difficulties"**: Ainsworth, "An Autobiographical Sketch," 455.

112 **the other women in Ainsworth's PhD cohort**: K. L. Isaacson, "Mary Ainsworth and John Bowlby: The Development of Attachment Theory" (unpublished doctoral dissertation, University of California, Davis, 2006), cited in Robbie Duschinsky, *Cornerstones of Attachment Research* (Oxford: Oxford Academic, 2020), 110, online edition, https://doi.org/10.1093/med-psych/9780198842064.001.0001.

112 **women married to men**: Richard Fry et al., "In a Growing Share of U.S. Marriages, Husbands and Wives Earn About the Same," Pew Research Center, April 14, 2023, https://www.pewresearch.org/social-trends/2023/04/13/in-a-growing-share-of-u-s-marriages-husbands-and-wives-earn-about-the-same/#-time-allocation-across-marriage-types.

113 **"small base"**: Karen, "Becoming Attached."

113 **Some mothers were seen**: Inge Bretherton, "The Origins of Attachment Theory: John Bowlby and Mary Ainsworth," *Developmental Psychology* 28, no. 5 (1992): 765.

114 **"I have been quite disappointed"**: Mary D. S. Ainsworth and Robert S. Marvin, "On the Shaping of Attachment Theory and Research: An Interview with Mary D. S. Ainsworth (Fall 1994)," *Monographs of the Society for Research in Child Development* 60, no. 2–3 (1995): 12.

115 **Ainsworth credited this method**: Duschinsky, *Cornerstones of Attachment Research*, 120–121.

116 **a woman named Barbara Wittig**: Duschinsky, *Cornerstones of Attachment Research*, 121.

117 **"freshness and vividness"**: Vicedo, *The Nature and Nurture of Love*, 201.

117 **Vicedo's analysis of the original records**: Marga Vicedo, "The Strange Situation of the Ethological Theory of Attachment: A Historical Perspective," in *The Cultural Nature of Attachment: Contextualizing Relationships and Development*, ed. Heidi Keller and Kim A. Bard (Cambridge, MA: MIT Press, 2017), 34.

123 **"the matriarch"**: Karen, "Becoming Attached."

123 **"She never had babies of her own"**: Maurer, "Never Miss an Opportunity to Hold a Baby."

123 **"the children I had vainly longed for"**: Maurer, "Never Miss an Opportunity to Hold a Baby."

124 **"It's very hard to become"**: Karen, "Becoming Attached," 17.

127 **"a huge scientific and civic campaign"**: Karen, "Becoming Attached," 17.

128 **the sociologist Patricia Hill Collins's research**: Patricia Hill Collins, "The Meaning of Motherhood in Black Culture and Black Mother/Daughter Relationships," *SAGE* 4, no. 2 (Fall 1987): 3–5.

128   **wage-earning is also an essential part:** Gabrielle Oliveira, *Motherhood Across Borders: Immigrants and Their Children in Mexico and New York* (New York: NYU Press, 2018); Gabrielle Oliveira, interview with Melissa Harris Perry, "What Does It Mean to Mother Across Borders?," May 6, 2022, in *The Takeaway*, podcast, https://www.wnycstudios.org/podcasts/takeaway/segments/mothers-across -borders.

128   **Black mothers have relied on the support of "othermothers":** Collins, "The Meaning of Motherhood," 5.

5. You Know More than You Think

131   **"When we have two hours":** Caitlin Moscatello, "Welcome to the Era of Very Earnest Parenting," *New York Times*, May 13, 2023, https://www.nytimes.com /2023/05/13/style/millennial-earnest-parenting.html.

133   **"confidence man":** Michael Zuckerman, "Dr. Spock: The Confidence Man," in *The Family in History*, ed. Charles E. Rosenberg (Philadelphia: University of Pennsylvania Press, 1975), 179–207.

133   **"king or queen of the house":** Thomas Maier, *Dr. Spock: An American Life* (New York: Harcourt Brace & Company, 1998), 9.

134   **"delicate constitution":** Maier, *Dr. Spock: An American Life*, 5.

134   **Hiddy remembered:** Maier, *Dr. Spock: An American Life*, 6.

134   **Spock's book sold more copies:** Rima D. Apple, *Perfect Motherhood: Science and Childrearing in America* (New Brunswick, NJ: Rutgers University Press, 2006), 117.

134   **He competed:** Maier, *Dr. Spock: An American Life*, 57.

134   **Mildred held a deep suspicion:** Maier, *Dr. Spock: An American Life*, 58.

135   **At Columbia:** Maier, *Dr. Spock: An American Life*, 77.

135   **it was actually Jane:** Maier, *Dr. Spock: An American Life*, 78.

135   **He began training:** Maier, *Dr. Spock: An American Life*, 93.

136   **an editor from Pocket Books:** Maier, *Dr. Spock: An American Life*, 124.

136   **She fact-checked:** Maier, *Dr. Spock: An American Life*, 126.

137   **she'd later insist:** Maier, *Dr. Spock: An American Life*, 380.

137   **he'd agreed to accept:** Maier, *Dr. Spock: An American Life*, 125.

138   **the book had sold:** Richard Bates, "Democratic Babies? Françoise Dolto, Benjamin Spock, and the Ideology of Post-War Parenting Advice," *Journal of Political Ideologies* 24, no. 2 (2019): 203.

138   **Spock's book outsold:** Bates, "Democratic Babies?," 203.

139   **"The Spockian mother":** Catherine A. Dobris et al., "The *Spockian Mother*: Images of the 'Good' Mother in Dr. Spock's *The Common Sense Book of Baby and Child Care*, 1946–1992," *Communication Quarterly* 65, no. 1 (2017): 47.

139   **"an emotional workday":** Nancy Pottishman Weiss, "Mother, the Invention of Necessity: Dr. Benjamin Spock's *Baby and Child Care*," *American Quarterly* 29, no. 5 (Winter 1977): 533.

144   **the average age:** Stephanie Coontz, *The Way We Never Were: American Families and the Nostalgia Trap* (New York: Basic Books, 1992), 24.

145   **many feared that once women:** Julia Grant, *Raising Baby by the Book: The Education of American Mothers* (New Haven, CT: Yale University Press, 1998), 20.

149   **"you are considered":** Maier, *Dr. Spock: An American Life*, 353.

150   **updating his books:** Grant, *Raising Baby by the Book*, 206.

150   **Women wrote to him:** Grant, *Raising Baby by the Book*, 206.

151   **Spock's books had positioned:** Dobris et al., "The *Spockian* Mother," 50.

151   **only a superficial revision:** Dobris et al., "The *Spockian* Mother," 51.

151   **The illustrations also confirm:** Dobris et al., "The *Spockian* Mother," 51.

151   **"every time a mother told me":** Grant, *Raising Baby by the Book*, 220.

152   **"women go out to work":** Deborah Blum, *Love at Goon Park: Harry Harlow and the Science of Affection* (New York: Basic Books, 2002), 235.

152   **"If you don't believe that God created":** Blum, *Love at Goon Park*, 237; Carol Tavris, "Harry, You Are Going to Go Down in History as the Father of the Cloth Mother," *Psychology Today*, April 1973.

152   **"the women followed me":** Jeannette DeWyze, "Childhood's End: Spock at 95," *San Diego Reader*, November 20, 1997.

153   **Spock's son Mike spoke up publicly:** Michael Spock, "My Father, Doctor Spock," *Ladies Home Journal*, May 1968.

154   **"through my writing, not my example":** Maier, *Dr. Spock: An American Life*, 455.

6. Many Warm, Friendly People

158   **"quite simple peoples":** Margaret Mead, *Coming of Age in Samoa: A Psychological Study of Primitive Youth for Western Civilization* (New York: Harper Perennial, 1928), 7.

158   **As Samoans since then:** Pulotu Peta Si'ulepa, "The Problems with Coming of Age: We Need to Tell Our Own Stories," season 6, episode 3, in *Sapiens*, hosted by Kate Ellis and Doris Tulifau, podcast, https://www.sapiens.org/culture/samoans-critique-margaret-mead/.

159   **When she married her first husband:** Charles King, *Gods of the Upper Air: How a Circle of Renegade Anthropologists Reinvented Race, Sex, and Gender in the Twentieth Century* (New York: Doubleday, 2019), 118.

159   **Though he'd initially been enthralled:** King, *Gods of the Upper Air*, 141.

160   **"The girl is going crazy":** King, *Gods of the Upper Air*, 142.

160   **"I have had a curious experience":** King, *Gods of the Upper Air*, 225.

160   **Mead met Benedict:** Lois W. Banner, *Intertwined Lives: Margaret Mead, Ruth Benedict, and Their Circle* (New York: Knopf, 2003), 180.

161   **the emerging discipline of anthropology:** King, *Gods of the Upper Air*, 118.

162   **when Mead and her newborn daughter:** Mary Catherine Bateson, *With a Daughter's Eye: A Memoir of Margaret Mead and Gregory Bateson* (New York: William Morrow & Co., 1984), 24.

162   **"more clearly herself":** Bateson, *With a Daughter's Eye*, 28.

162   **She was determined to breastfeed:** Elesha J. Coffman, "The Margaret Mead Problem," *Aeon*, July 1, 2021, https://aeon.co/essays/when-it-came-to-sex-and

-gender-margaret-mead-had-it-both-ways; Nancy Lutkehaus, *Margaret Mead: The Making of an American Icon* (Princeton, NJ: Princeton University Press, 2008), 64.

163   **She'd met him:** Lutkehaus, *Margaret Mead*, 64.

164   **"In my family":** Bateson, *With a Daughter's Eye*, 20.

164   **Subsequent researchers and Samoans:** For a discussion of the reception of Mead's work among Samoans and the calls for Samoans to document their own culture, see Kate Ellis and Doris Tulifau, "The Problems with Coming of Age," season 6, in *Sapiens*, podcast, https://www.sapiens.org/podcast-season/season-6/.

166   **"my most rewarding intellectual experience":** World Health Organization, *Report on the Meetings of the Study Group on the Psychobiological Development of the Child* (Geneva: World Health Organization, 1958), 13, accessed December 18, 2023, https://policycommons.net/artifacts/611122/report-on-the-meetings-of-the-study-group-on-the-psychobiological-development-of-the-child/1590740/.

166   **by blithely asserting:** Frank C. P. van der Horst et al., "A Tale of Four Countries: How Bowlby Used His Trip Through Europe to Write the WHO Report and Spread His Ideas," *Journal of the History of the Behavioral Sciences* 56, no. 3 (Summer 2020): 173, doi:10.1002/jhbs.22016.

166   **He cited Mead only once:** Marga Vicedo, "The Strange Situation of the Ethological Theory of Attachment: A Historical Perspective," in *The Cultural Nature of Attachment: Contextualizing Relationships and Development*, ed. Heidi Keller and Kim A. Bard (Cambridge, MA: MIT Press, 2017), 18.

167   **"deprivation occurring without physical separation":** Mary Ainsworth, "The Effects of Maternal Deprivation: A Review of Findings and Controversy in the Context of Research Strategy," *Public Health Papers* 14 (1962): 143.

167   **Mead made the practical point:** Margaret Mead, "Some Theoretical Considerations on the Problem of Mother-Child Separation," *American Journal of Orthopsychiatry* 24, no. 3 (1954): 471–483.

168   **"many warm, friendly people":** Margaret Mead, "A Cultural Anthropologist's Approach to Maternal Deprivation," in *Deprivation of Maternal Care: A Reassessment of Its Effects* (Geneva: World Health Organization, 1962), 55.

168   **When researchers looked again:** Sarah Blaffer Hrdy, *Mothers and Others: The Evolutionary Origins of Mutual Understanding* (Cambridge, MA: Harvard University Press, 2011), 73–75.

168   **And recent studies in anthropology:** Nikhil Chaudhary, Gul Deniz Salali, and Annie Swanepoel, "Sensitive Responsiveness and Multiple Caregiving Networks Among Mbendjele BaYaka Hunter-Gatherers: Potential Implications for Psychological Development and Well-being," *Developmental Psychology* 60, no. 3 (November 2023), doi:10.1037/dev0001601; and Abigail E. Page et al., "Children Are Important Too: Juvenile Playgroups and Maternal Childcare in a Foraging Population, the Agta," *Philosophical Transactions of the Royal Society B* 376, no. 1827 (May 3, 2021), https://doi.org/10.1098/rstb.2020.0026.

169   **One attachment theory researcher notes:** Robbie Duschinsky, *Cornerstones of Attachment Research* (Oxford: Oxford Academic, 2020), 182, online edition, https://doi.org/10.1093/med-psych/9780198842064.001.0001.

172   **Making parental leave available:** Hillary Frank, "It's a Real Mother, Part 4: Leave," November 29, 2017, in *Longest Shortest Time*, podcast, https://longestshortesttime.com/episode-145-its-a-real-mother-part-4-leave; and Brigid Schulte et al., "Paid Family Leave: How Much Time Is Enough?," *Better Life Lab*, June 16, 2017, https://www.newamerica.org/better-life-lab/reports/paid-family-leave-how-much-time-enough/.

174   **Catherine would remember later:** Bateson, *With a Daughter's Eye*, 38.

175   **And when the United States entered:** King, *Gods of the Upper Air*, 313.

175   **Catherine says she remembers those summers:** Bateson, *With a Daughter's Eye*, 38.

176   **Catherine remarked that it was only later:** Bateson, *With a Daughter's Eye*, 68.

176   **"Margaret and Gregory both spent long hours":** Bateson, *With a Daughter's Eye*, 66.

176   **"There were all these beloved people":** Bateson, *With a Daughter's Eye*, 39.

177   **"She set out to create a community":** Bateson, *With a Daughter's Eye*, 16.

182   **And while her advice:** Paul Shankman, "The Public Anthropology of Margaret Mead: *Redbook*, Women's Issues, and the 1960s," *Current Anthropology* 59, no. 1 (February 2018): 57.

182   **It was ideas like these:** Betty Friedan, *The Feminine Mystique: 50th Anniversary Edition* (New York: W. W. Norton & Company, 2013), 154.

182   **Mead's advice evolved:** Shankman, "The Public Anthropology of Margaret Mead," 62.

182   **It wasn't until the mid-1970s:** Shankman, "The Public Anthropology of Margaret Mead," 62.

7. Relearning the Nature of Love

190   **"She sat all that time":** Deborah Blum, *Love at Goon Park: Harry Harlow and the Science of Affection* (New York: Basic Books, 2002), 229.

190   **Peggy devised an experimental setup:** Blum, *Love at Goon Park*, 202–203; and G. C. Ruppenthal et al., "Development of Peer Interactions in Monkeys Raised in a Nuclear-Family Environment," *Child Development* 45, no. 3 (1974): 670–682.

191   **His work was cited in a *Redbook* article:** Blum, *Love at Goon Park*, 175.

193   **there are lots of ways to raise a healthy child:** See, for example, Sara Harkness's review essay, "The Strange Situation of Attachment Research: A Review of Three Books," *Reviews in Anthropology* 44 (2015): 178–197, for a helpful overview of cross-cultural ethnographic studies of childhood.

193   **she continued working and teaching:** Frances K. Graham, Kai Jensen, and Leon J. Yarrow, "In Memoriam: Margaret Kuenne Harlow," *Child Development* 42, no. 5 (November 1971): 1314.

193   **Harry was angry about that:** Blum, *Love at Goon Park*, 228.

195   **"my mom was the one who loved me"**: Blum, *Love at Goon Park*, 251.

198   **"We don't care for children because"**: Alison Gopnik, *The Gardener and the Carpenter: What the New Science of Child Development Tells Us About the Relationship Between Parents and Children* (New York: Farrar, Strauss & Giroux, 2016), 87.

202   **Kawan, the orangutan at the zoo in Madison:** Kawan's prenatal care is described in an article from the University of Wisconsin–Madison's news service: Nicholas Brigham Schmuhl, "Zoo's Mother-to-Be Receives Prenatal Care from UW-Affiliated Health Professionals," February 18, 2015, https://news.wisc.edu/zoos-mother-to-be-receives-prenatal-care-from-uw-affiliated-health-professionals/. Details about Keju's birth and Kawan's struggle with parenting come from articles in *The Isthmus* and the *Wisconsin State Journal*: Peter Jurich, "Waiting for Keju," *The Isthmus*, August 20, 2015, https://isthmus.com/news/news/vilas-zookeepers-work-to-reunite-rejected-baby-orangutan-wit/; Bill Novak, "Baby Orangutan Keju Born at Vilas Zoo," *Wisconsin State Journal*, April 23, 2015, https://madison.com/news/local/baby-orangutan-keju-born-at-vilas-zoo/article_8e46fc6f-376b-5200-afba-cc6ca55dc268.html; and Bill Novak, "Farewell to Keju: Baby Orangutan Snubbed by Mom, Moving to Atlanta," *Wisconsin State Journal*, October 16, 2015, https://madison.com/news/local/farewell-to-keju-baby-orangutan-snubbed-by-mom-moving-to/article_0524d61a-989c-5b20-a802-0bc30368ee1d.html.

Coda: "Love Is Not a Given but a Gift"

215   **In the early fifties, when Seymour Levine:** Deborah Blum, *Love at Goon Park: Harry Harlow and the Science of Affection* (New York: Basic Books, 2002), 179–182.

217   **I think of an essay a friend wrote:** Chloe Benjamin, as told to Danielle Cohen, "The High Point of My Career Came with a Physical Breakdown," *The Cut*, March 9, 2022, https://www.thecut.com/2022/03/chloe-benjamin-the-immortalists-ambition-migraines.html?utm_campaign=nym&utm_source=tw&utm_medium=s1.

218   **"Maternal love is not a given but a gift":** Nan Robertson, "The 'Myth' of Mother Love Is Challenged," *New York Times*, November 16, 1981, https://www.nytimes.com/1981/11/16/style/the-myth-of-mother-love-is-challenged.html.

Index

ABOUT THE AUTHOR

Missie Jurick

Nancy Reddy's previous books include the poetry collections *Pocket Universe* and *Double Jinx*, a winner of the National Poetry Series competition. With Emily Pérez, she's coeditor of *The Long Devotion: Poets Writing Motherhood.* Her essays have appeared in *Slate, Poets & Writers, Romper, The Millions,* and elsewhere. The recipient of grants from the New Jersey State Council on the Arts and the Sustainable Arts Foundation and a Walter E. Dakin Fellowship from the Sewanee Writers' Conference, she teaches writing at Stockton University and publishes the newsletter *Write More, Be Less Careful.*